TAKE YOUR STAND

RAISE STRONG CHILDREN WHO CAN GUARD AGAINST DECEPTION AND STAND FOR TRUTH

Susan Elaine Perez

Education Empowerment Coach

"These are the commands, decrees, and laws that the LORD your God directed me to teach you ... so that you, and your children, and their children after them may fear the LORD your God as long as you live by keeping all His decrees and commands ... so that you may enjoy a long life."

Deuteronomy 6: 1-2 NIV

Printed and published in the United States of America by Susan Elaine Perez

2023 © by Susan Elaine Perez
ISBN 9798851796371

Scripture references are from the following public domain sources:

The King James Version (KJV). Public Domain.

The New American Standard Bible (NASB) © 1960, 1962, 1963, 1972, 1972, 1973, E1975, and 1977 by the Lockman Foundation. Used by permission.

The New International Version of the Bible (NIV) © 1873, 1978, 1984, 2011 by Biblica, Inc. Used by permission of Zondervan Bible Publishers.

The New Living Translation (NLT) © 1996, 2004, 2015 by Tyndale House Foundation. Used by permission of Tyndale House Publishers. All rights reserved.

The World English Bible (WEB). Public Domain.

Disclaimers

None of the information in this book is intended to be medical advice. The content is educational opinion based on personal years of experience. The author has no affiliation with any of the resources or apps suggested.

The recommended resources were good quality and beneficial at the time of this book's publication. It is important for YOU, as parents, to do your own research and consideration to see if these continue to be quality resources and apps. You must determine whether they are suitable for your child.

If you find mistakes or other quality resources, please let us know. We want this book to be a service to God with the best information possible. edempower777@gmail.com

Note: This book will interchange "he" and "she," "him" and "her" as the skills and ideas apply to both sexes.

TABLE OF CONTENTS
PART 1

PART 2

If you need help for yourself and your children to be able to take a stand for your family's Christian values in education and in the world, contact us for a free 1-on-1 Strategy Session: edempower777@gmail.com

Education Empowerment Coach
Susan Perez

DEDICATION WITH LOVE

To Harley, Peyton, and Leia (my three grandchildren):

May you be able to stand strong with grace

and meekness (harnessed strength)

for yourselves; for others;

for important issues; and for things that are right,

like David and Joseph and Esther in the Bible,

– with God on your side!

Bless Your Child

24 "The Lord bless you
and keep you;
25 the Lord make his face shine on you
and be gracious to you;
26 the Lord turn his face toward you
and give you peace."

Numbers 6:24-26 New International Version

PART 1

This section of this parenting book shares a story of struggles, along with some workable solutions, that a family goes through in raising their three children. Hopefully, parents can relate to and even learn from these life-like stories.

CHAPTER 1
THE FIRST 5 YEARS ARE KEY!

The first 5 years of children's development are critical to their health, well-being, and overall path for life. Fortunately, there are many things that parents can do to *"Train up a child in the way that he should go"* (Proverbs 22:6 NASB) and to help direct his path. This especially includes the spiritual and age-appropriate responsibility aspects of development in raising STRONG CHILDREN who learn to fend for themselves and help others in the world.

How will children ever be strong enough to be IN this world but not OF the world?

PART 1 is an example of some struggles and some solutions that families go through in raising their children. Hopefully parents can relate to and even learn from these 'life-like encounters.'

Don't miss PART 2!

PART 2 is a resource that parents can refer to every few months at first, and then later, once or twice each year to see how their child is developing in the areas listed. Please pay special attention to **Spiritual Development** (which starts with two scriptures to memorize with your child) and **Responsibility Measures** (that a strong child can be expected to do at each age).

There are many Parenting Tips and Related Stories included as well.

As a little bonus tucked into the PART 2 pages, **<u>Gift Ideas</u>** for birthday and Christmas are included for each age.

Note: This book will interchange "he" and "she," "him" and "her" as the skills and ideas apply to both sexes.

CHAPTER 2
WHAT A MESS!

How will our children ever be strong enough to be IN this world, but not OF the world?

What are parents to do about a world that is trying to indoctrinate and sexualize our children?

"I just don't get it!" Project Manager Carol exclaimed to her friend Penny after a very productive team planning session. "How is it we can come to work and sit down with all different people at our team meeting, brainstorm, divvy up responsibilities, set timelines, and know the work will be done and ready to discuss next week, but at home, I can't even get my children's attention much less get them to straighten up?"

"Well, maybe it's because we don't have TVs here," Penny responded glibly.

Carol stood stupefied in her light bulb moment. "Good grief – you may be right!"

After an awkward silence of contemplation, Carol spoke up again. "But here the team respects me, listens, and responds to everything I throw at them."

"Well, we do respect you, but we're always on guard, because you also control whether we get to continue drawing a paycheck. Also, we may be a little afraid of you, or you may call us out in front of this team. That breeds motivation to do our best!" Penny replied.

"Wow! That's a profound comment. Thank you for it, I guess! But I can't fire my kids. I'm stuck with them." Carol gathered up her meeting notes and pens and notepad as Penny cleared the long conference table.

"Are there things you can do to demand or command their respect, or at least call their bluff? Are they afraid of you, at least a little?" Penny asked from her experience of raising 4 boys.

"That is something Ron and I need to discuss!" Carol finished putting everything into her workbag.

"How's it going with Katie now that she's in, let's see, 5th grade, right?" Penny quizzed.

"I can't believe some of the things she comes up with. Sometimes I feel like we're losing her. I'm not sure if she even believes in our family's Christian values any more. She talks about people going trans like it's the popular topic now, but that's a whole 'nother topic for a different day," Penny's jaw dropped, but she tried to mask her shock as they headed toward the door.

"I've got to get to the daycare to pick up little Jack. Thanks for asking, Penny. We'll talk later, OK?" Carol looked at Penny appreciatively and scooted out of the meeting room, down the hall to her office, and then out of the parking lot.

Once they arrived home, Carol put on her happy face, "Come help Mommy make supper, Jackie!" She started to put the 10-month-old in the highchair. Her breasts stinging, she realized she still had to breastfeed Jack.

In the toy room, Carol eyed the storm all around her as she sat nursing little Jack. A race car in his hand fell to the floor among a myriad of other toys. Older son Alex, 5, had left several piles of books around the room as well. Carol felt closed in, trapped, helpless. She closed her eyes and breathed a heavy sigh as she thought,

I know we decided we would nurse Jack longer, maybe even 12 months or more, after we read this had worked well for a mom who took away one feeding at a time. It might be about time to take away the 5 p.m. feeding so I can make supper when I get home from work. I'll talk to Ron about it tonight.

Just as she finished, she heard Ron's car pull into the garage. She bent down to hug Alex as he ran in from T-ball practice, still sweaty. "How was practice?"

"I had a good hit! And I got to run to third base!"

"Wow, that's great!" Carol bragged.

"Is supper almost ready?" Ron asked over the mayhem of Alex and little Jack, already revving up their race cars in the toy room.

Carol felt a little guilty that dinner wasn't yet ready. "It will be ready soon," she called a bit defensively.

"Will you be able to make it to Alex's T-ball game tomorrow afternoon?" Carol asked as she stirred the simmering pasta. "He gets so excited when he sees you there!"

"We'll see how the day goes tomorrow," Ron answered while sifting through the mail that had piled up.

Carol drained the noodles, added the jar of alfredo sauce, and put grilled chicken strips onto a plate, as her stomach growled.

"Supper is ready! Wash up and come eat!"

Alex came running. Ron sauntered in.

"Did you wash up?" she asked Alex as she put Jack in his highchair and got out his baby food.

Once they all sat down, Ron led the prayer as the family put their hands together. "Dear God, Thank you for this food, and for our family. Keep us safe and help us to be obedient. In Jesus Name, Amen."

Alex had even repeated some of the prayer, Carol noticed lovingly, but at the same time, she bit her lip to avoid talking about the mess in the next room.

Meanwhile, Katie strolled in from the carpool that had just dropped her off after gymnastics. The pink streaks in her blond hair bobbed up and down. "That coach is so lame," Katie griped as she dropped her backpack. "He won't even let Jane and me hold hands at practice. He says it's not the time or place, but kids do it at school."

Carol saw Ron's jaw tense up.

"Sometimes I just think I should be a boy!" Katie blurted out. "Some of my friends are going trans!"

Yikes! Carol screamed mentally as her stomach turned somersaults! *I can hardly ponder that crazy comment! What are we going to do?*

She teared up.

Email <u>edempower777@gmail.com</u> for your free gift of "What to Do When Your Child Asks about Transgender Issues?"

CHAPTER 3

WE'D BETTER GET ORGANIZED!

Carol appreciated the evening quiet time that she and Ron had committed to having together, especially to pray for their family.

"Jack does seem calmer than Katie and Alex," she analyzed. "It is probably from nursing him this long. Maybe it **is** making a difference, but what if I give up the 5 p.m. feeding now that he's 10 months old and so active?" Carol fingered her Bible looking at Ron.

After a pause, "I think it is time," Ron agreed.

"Hey, what do you think we can do about the constant mess around this house, especially in the toy room?" Carol sighed, intentionally avoiding the subject of Katie's comment at dinner.

"Should we set up a routine?" Ron questioned.

"What kind of routine?" Carol asked.

"Well, we could figure out where we want each toy to go and take pictures to put on the front of the drawer like that book 'Raising Strong Children' suggests." Ron sounded hopeful.

"Will you help to get that done?" Carol wondered out loud.

"Yes, if you'll help me to enforce it consistently."

"Well, I guess we'd better do something, or the next 17 years are going to be drudgery," Carol responded.

"Now that we're coming up with a plan for organization, consistency in carrying it out is the key," Ron added. "Con - sis - ten - cy," he clarified and affirmed.

"Also, we need to keep praying to figure out what to do about Katie and her craziness over all the trans stuff. Soon we've gotta face this problem head on."

CHAPTER 4

WE'VE GOT A PLAN!

"OK, how are we going to do this?" Carol eyed the junkyard scene of the toy room.

"Hmmm," Ron mused. "Well, first, what if we remove, maybe donate, some of the toys the kids don't use any more?

Then, we can take photos of 2 or 3 of each kind of toy that they do still like to play with. Let's use the pictures of their toys to label each drawer the toys go in. I think we can fit 6 or 8 pictures like that on a page and then print them out."

"Yeah! That's a great idea! Then let's use clear packaging tape on the photos as labels for each drawer and cubby. Like right here. Take a picture of the stethoscope and then we'll write Medical Toys after we print it out," Carol added enthusiastically, even though it was already 10 p.m. after a long day at work.

"Let's put the animals over here." Ron dumped handfuls of rubber, 4-legged buddies into the second drawer.

"The race cars will fit here. We don't actually have to put them all up. Let's just figure out where they will go and get each drawer and cubby labeled," Carol suggested. "Tomorrow we can help the kids actually put the toys into the right places."

"I think you should order a net that I can hang in this corner for all of the stuffed animals," Ron said as he created a 3-foot-tall pile of soft pals.

"We may need to put some in a bag, make them absent for awhile, and donate 'em to a shelter. There's just no way 2 little boys need that many stuffed animals." Carol stepped over the pile.

"Let's put Alex's books in these 4 sections of the shelves and teach him how to turn them the right side up with the title showing on each binding," Ron analyzed as he pushed the books to one side of the room.

"We need to use the toy box for something else so there's not 15 different kinds of toys in there now that everything is going to have its own drawer or cubby," Carol added.

"OK. I think I have all the pictures. Let's print them out and get 'em taped on, pronto, so we can go to bed," Ron responded as he headed to the printer.

"This will help our trio learn to clean up and keep things organized. Let's ask Katie to help us train the boys so she takes some responsibility for this project," Carol said as she grabbed the packaging tape and started writing a word or two with a black marker to label each picture.

Ron taped each photo/label onto the appropriate drawer or cubby.

"I guess we can tell the kids about this plan tomorrow night at dinner and tweak it as we go if we need to," Ron yawned while heading to bed.

CHAPTER 5

THE COMPETITION

The next evening at supper, Ron explained the plan. "After we all put our dishes into the dishwasher and clean up from supper, we are going to have a competition!"

"What kind of competition?" Alex quizzed as Katie rolled her eyes in dismay.

"Everyone is going to help 'zip' up the house," Carol chimed in.

Ron added, "This will be a fun competition to see who can pick up the most things in 15 minutes and get their area 'zipped up,' but we're not just picking up our own things. We are paying attention and picking everything that is out of place."

"We'll start off playing the song Zippedy Do Dah to get us going," Carol said cheerfully. "Any other suggestions for fast-paced songs while cleaning up to make it more fun?"

Katie named a couple of excellent songs to play.

"OK, let's get going," Dad said as Mom started the music.

"No-o-o-o," Jack said and sat down in the middle of the room with the toy cars all around him.

Carol pulled Baby Jack up and helped him and Alex put their toys in the proper places. She noticed Alex was playing.

"Come on, Alex. Put the medical toys in this drawer with the picture of the stethoscope." He acted like he didn't hear her. "Alex!" she raised her voice. Then he throttled into gear.

Ron checked on the kids, including Katie, to make sure they were racing around and doing their best work. He also straightened up as he went.

Carol heard him brag, "Katie, good job in your room. Can you help me in the TV room for a few minutes? And please take these dishes to the kitchen."

"But they're not mine," whined Katie.

"That doesn't matter," Dad said. "We are a team here, straightening up all the house for 15 minutes, not just our own stuff. You're a big help to this family. We need you to help as well. Just 'til the timer goes off."

She let out a big sigh, "O-o-okay." Katie dragged her feet, but took the dishes to the kitchen.

The timer went off, and Carol stopped the music. She and Ron spent a few minutes bragging about each of the kids and let them tell what they had picked up before they headed to bath time.

Once the kids were in bed, Ron and Carol headed to their own room for their increasingly cherished quiet time.

CHAPTER 6
QUIET TIME AND REFLECTION

"How do you think 'Zipping up the house' is going?" Carol asked Ron a few days later at their nightly quiet time together.

"Not too bad," he answered. "I mean, there have been a couple of nights that we just didn't have time before bedtime, but I think the kids are starting to get the hang of this new habit."

"For sure the house seems more organized. Labeling the drawers and cubbies was a great idea. It really helps," Carol chimed in as she stifled a yawn.

"I think we need to pray fervently for Katie and ask for wisdom on how to draw her back to our Christian values," Ron mused. "Maybe we should start reading a few Bible verses at supper and talk about them. Or memorize a scripture."

"Or both. Would we have to come up with the material ourselves?" Carol wondered as she stopped brushing her hair for a moment.

"Let's ask friends at church to see who has some ideas," Ron said with measure. "There is wisdom in the counsel of many."

"Let's also pray that we do a better job with Alex and Jack so they become strong Christians early in life and can take a stand for their biblical values," Carol added. And then, she prayed exactly that.

CHAPTER 7

NOW THAT YOU'RE IN SCHOOL

"Hey, Alex," Ron said during dinnertime. "We want to talk about your being in kindergarten. "Katie, what do you think he should watch out for?"

Katie looked at him surprised.

"I mean, how do we make sure he is not being taught things that we don't approve of?" Ron added. "It just seems like we hear more and more being taught at school that kids don't need to be thinking about yet. Not reading, writing and 'rithmetic, but other stuff they bring up."

"Well, I guess he should just come tell you if there is something that makes him feel uncomfortable," Katie twisted her pink hair as she talked.

"Like what?" asked Alex.

"Maybe anything about boys not wanting to be boys," explained Carol.

"Or girls not thinking they should be a girl anymore," added Ron.

Katie rolled her eyes and strategized, "What about evolution?" to change the subject.

"What's that?" Alex asked.

"Well, it's a theory – never proven – that mentions apes becoming humans," Ron simplified.

"Really? How does that happen?" Alex quipped as his eyes perked up.

"Well, it doesn't," Dad said. "That's the point. God made us, but a man named Darwin tried to make it seem like we all came from a soup."

"Sounds big-time crazy," Alex popped up.

"Exactly," Carol laughed. "I guess Katie is right. If something makes you feel uncomfortable at school – now I don't mean you could get out of doing your work or anything – but if you think there is something we for sure wouldn't approve of, please come tell us so we can talk about it."

"And we will ask you from time to time. We will want to know what you're reading, as you start learning to read," Ron said as he picked up his empty plate and headed to the sink.

Everyone else followed as they finished their last bites.

CHAPTER 8
DO WE SPANK?

Carol: "Sometimes I can't get Jack to pick up his toys. Is he too young to spank?"

"Well, after telling him twice to pick it up, let's try taking his hand and walking him over to the toy," Ron answered. "If he won't pick it up, just pull his hand down to the toy and grab it together with him if necessary, in order to make him pick it up. Then walk him over to where it goes while reminding him where to put it. We can't let him get away with not minding this young. Makes me shiver to think what he'd be like in middle school!

"Good idea," Carol smiled. "Remember how it's affected Katie. You know that we let her get away with some things when she was his age. We can't repeat that mistake. Let's learn from it instead."

"Yeah! We're going to have to work twice as hard now to brag on what Katie does well and give her some responsibility and hold her accountable," Carol said as she put away her Bible that they had been reading from.

"Can we spend some time praying about all of this?" Ron suggested.

CHAPTER 9

SHARING

"That's my toy," Alex yelled.

"NO! Mine," Little Jack yelled back as he twisted away to keep Alex from getting the toy.

"It's mine," Alex yelled louder.

"OK guys, who had it first?" Katie refereed as she stepped into the room.

"Jack did, but it's my toy car," Alex snapped back.

"Well, let him play with it for little while since he already had it, and then see if you can get him interested in something else," Katie advised.

Alex reluctantly reached for some toy animals, and bingo! Jack's attention switched. As soon as he dropped the toy car, Alex retrieved it.

"Mine," cried Jack.

"You stopped playing with it, Jack, so it is Alex's turn now. You can play with it later," Carol hollered over Jack's crying.

"Let's play with the animal sounds," Carol picked that toy up. "Can you pull the string? Oh, what animal is that?" she added enthusiastically to get Jack's attention.

"Mine, mine, mine, Mommy!" Jack whimpered while reaching for Alex's toy car. This time Alex jerked away.

"OK, boys, I will put ALL of them up if you can't share," Carol stated firmly as she crossed her arms and waited. Alex offered the toy car to Jack for another turn and started to play with some animals again. But before too long, little Jack was happily playing with the animals as well.

CHAPTER 10

LET'S PLAY

"Hey everyone, since it's Saturday, let's get out the Play-Doh!" Carol exclaimed as she watched Jack and Alex absorbed in TV. They barely even looked her way, so Carol got out the Play-Doh and switched off the TV with the remote. Now she had both boys' attention. "Katie, do you want to join us?"

Katie had earphones in, so Carol had to go over and shake her gently to get Katie's attention. "Hey, come play Play-Doh with us! The boys love it when you make interesting figures and tell them stories." Somehow, this captured Katie's creative streak. She slid slowly off the couch and joined the family at the kids' table in the toy room.

Katie began making a menagerie of animals. Usually, the rule for using Play-Doh was only one color at a time, but ever since Katie turned 10 and was very careful not to mix the colors as she put it away, she got to use several colors at a time.

"Neigh, neigh," Katie's brown horse said as it galloped all over the table and up Little Jack's head and shoulders, making him giggle with delight.

"Moo, moo," said her white and black spotted cow as it confronted Alex head on.

Carol watched in delight as Katie started telling a story of farm animals that resembled 'Old MacDonald' without actually being the song. Jack and Alex were familiar enough with the song that they could predict and join in on some of Katie's animal sounds in the story.

The tale absorbed them as it unfolded. Mom rolled out a green snake and pressed the end for its head just as Katie swept up the "green, vicious snake hissed at the horse which reared up, pawed the ground and eyed the snake with fright." Katie spun in dramatic details to her story!

Carol praised God quietly as Katie continued to be a part of the family – a team leader at this point – and entertain the excited little listeners.

Back from his morning golf outing with the guys, Ron glowed at what he saw. Carol noticed that his eyes lit up as he watched the family playing together. The TVs and earphones were off as they had discussed a few nights ago, with ALL three children involved. Everyone neighed and mooed and giggled. Ron put away his things and watched, adding a few animal sounds of his own with a grin on his face.

CHAPTER 11

RESTLESS

"Little Jack, why are you so restless?" Carol looked up from her phone as she gave Jack his bottle.

Squirming this way and that, he looked at her and tried to twist out of her lap.

"Are you outgrowing your nap time? Surely not!" Carol pondered out loud.

She grabbed a book and read 'Bear Hunt,' singing the parts she knew.

Jack settled in and drank more of his bottle. His little feet popped straight up, almost hitting Carol in the head.

"What was that?" Carol admonished rather sternly.

She gave him a good hug and declared, "Jesus loves you and so do I."

Jack snuggled in again. His brown eyes searched his Momma for 'she's mine' reassurance like kids sometimes do when no one sees them. She admired his little tuft of brown hair curled over on the top of his head.

Again, Jack squirmed. His little legs, very strong now, pushed against Carol's thighs and fighting to be free.

Carol smelled the problem. "Awww, you're dirty." She paused the feeding to change his stinky diaper and tie it inside a small grocery sack to contain the smell.

Back in the rocker with little Jack, she sang "Jesus Loves Me" as she returned the bottle to his mouth. His eyes sagged even though he still struggled against sleep.

She sang "Jesus Loves the Little Children" and "Go Tell It on the Mountain" and a few other songs. She reached over and gently stroked his eyebrow, which resulted in his little eyes closing. Within a few seconds, the almost-empty bottle slipped out of his mouth. She put him on her shoulder, patted out a burp, and then laid him in his crib for naptime.

A few solitary moments had arrived at last as she turned on the radio to a Christian music station to block out noise of the older children. With a silent twist of the doorknob, Carol slipped out of the room with a sigh.

CHAPTER 12
SHOULD WE LET HIM QUIT?

"This game is so close!" said Carol to her friend Carmen as they watched their boys playing T-ball.

"Hey, get outta the mud!" Carol ordered as she hopped out of the bleachers to grab Jack before too much squishy grime damaged his relatively new tennies.

"Come on, boys! We just need one more run to win!" Carmen yelled at the team as her son hit the ball off of the tee and headed to first base.

"Come on Alex! You can do it!" Carol encouraged as Alex grabbed his bat and swung it several times like the guys in the big leagues do.

Alex swung and missed. "Come on, son!" Ron encouraged. Alex looked around and smiled to see his dad.

"Swing, buddy, buddy. Swing, buddy," called his coach.

Alex did swing again, but the ball plopped just a few feet from the tee. "Run!" The crowd roared.

Alex launched toward first, but tripped before he got there. He skidded, fell, and scratched his outstretched hands. He hopped up and bolted at the base. The next scene wasn't pretty as the first baseman picked up the ball, turned a half circle, and plopped his foot onto the bag right before Alex got there.

"Awww!" the crowd roared as the last chance for the team to win this game slipped away.

"Way to fall, Alex!" his teammates teased as he entered the dugout. Alex looked down at his feet, 100% dejected.

"Hey!" the coach corrected them. "We're all in this together. We win some and we lose some. Let's line up to give them high fives. No negative talk!" Coach Rudy eyed the team with a stern stare.

After that, Alex grabbed his glove and bat and headed to the car. He slumped in the back seat. As everybody climbed in, Alex declared, "I'm gonna quit! This is no fun!"

Ron looked at Carol and said, "You can quit when the season is over, but not now. You must finish out the commitment you made to yourself, to your team, to your coach, and to good sportsmanship when you signed up.

Heading home they discussed that if Alex chose the easy way out – not to play next year – he'd have to pick something else to get involved in and develop his skills.

"You can't just sit at home and play video games," Carol added.

Still ticked off and out of sorts, Alex just looked out the car window.

After a long silence, Ron added, "You've actually been showing pretty good form lately. That's really important in the long run. I mean, you probably don't realize how much you have improved. Coach Rudy said the same thing when he talked to us after the game. He also likes that you get along with everyone and have good team spirit."

"We're really proud of you for that!" Carol added. "You'll get over this rough spot. We've all been there."

CHAPTER 13
RAISING STRONG CHRISTIANS

Ron looked at Carol, "I appreciate these evening quiet times we decided to have. What are we going to do about Katie and the worldly views she seems to be developing? Can we pray about that, how to approach this, and hopefully keep her secure in faith?"

Carol replied, "Yes! I am still so concerned. This challenge is important."

After a fervent prayer time together Carol analyzed, "Maybe for our next dinner discussion we can talk about what traits we should look for in a friend, and what traits we should have in order to be a good friend. We've never talked about that."

"Let's look for related scripture as well." Ron added. "This is an ongoing prayer for us, to guard our children from a worldly point of view. Isn't there a scripture that says something like 'We are to be IN the world, but not OF the world?'"

"I guess we need to learn all about how to develop a biblical world view," Carol suggested. "Not sure exactly where, but I believe I've read that the reason young adults stray away from God and from church is because they don't believe that every word of the Bible is true. Honey, do you believe that every word of the Bible is true?"

There was a thoughtful pause.

"Well, I don't believe that God makes mistakes. We need to look into this further," Ron pledged. "This search and discussion might continue as long as our children are at home with us. We need to add this to things we pray about for years to come."

"I agree," Carol nodded and smiled. "For sure, and every day, we need to keep a close eye on Jack and Alex so they don't forget our family's Christian values like Katie seems to slip away from sometimes."

CHAPTER 14

WHAT IS A FRIEND?

"Tonight let's talk about what a good friend is." Ron explained at the dinner table. "Katie, what would you look for in a friend."

"Don't 'xactly know what you mean," she quipped.

"I mean what would you want your friends to be like?"

"Well, they should be nice. I guess I would want someone that is honest, and treated equal to me," Katie said with a wrinkled forehead. "For sure not bossing me around, and not expecting me to come up with all of the ideas either. I think that helps it to be more fun."

"What about you, Alex?" Ron switched his gaze.

"Hmmm, good at baseball. Gots lots of toys,"

"Has. Has lots of toys," Carol corrected.

"Has lots of fun stuff to play with. Not mean. Sticks up for me," Alex finished and smiled as he answered.

"What about you, Mom?" Dad continued.

"Well, a friend should put up with me even when we don't agree. Respect differences, and for sure not try to make me be like them. I really prefer Christian friends, because then I know that we basically believe the same things, and we both use the Bible. We learn from the same book.

"We use the two most important things – the Bible and prayer – as guides for decisions and the way we act. Want to hear a verse that sums it up for me?"

"Sure," they said.

"Love is patient and kind. Love is not jealous or boastful or proud, or rude. It does not demand its own way."

I prefer friends that don't insist on having their own way," Carol looked up.

"It is not irritable, and keeps no record of being wronged. It does not rejoice about injustice, but rejoices whenever truth wins out. Love never gives up, never loses faith, is always hopeful, and endures through every circumstance!" Corinthians 13: 4-7 (NLT)

"That's a good summary," Ron added. "You know your friends are really important. They can either help you become better or pull you down.

"I remember when I was younger, I had a friend who tempted me several times to do some bad things. One time he wanted me to get into a fight with him. He jumped another guy and wanted me to help him win. Then he was going to steal a car. Good thing I had football practice so I couldn't go with him.

"He also drank before he was old enough, even got some of us other guys to join in a few times 'til the cops showed up at a party one time. Again, good thing I wasn't there, but a couple of football players were, and they got kicked off the football team, as they should have.

"That was it for me. I quit hanging out with him after that. I wonder what he's up to these days?

"Here's another good Bible verse," Ron said, thumbing through his Bible.

"In 1 Corinthians 15:33 (NIV) it says, *'Do not be misled: Bad company corrupts good character.'*"

Ron finished reading and looked up. "So, good friends leave a positive influence, but bad friends can help lead you astray. You have to be careful who you hang out with,"

"OK, got that part. But how can you tell if someone really is a good friend?" Katie asked.

"Well, there are the basic things like 'A friend loves at all times.' So if you are upset, they will probably ask what is wrong or give you encouragement, be a good listener, or just give you some space if you need it for a while, if they are a true friend," Mom said.

"A true friend will look for opportunities to express love and keep the friendship going. Good friends will stand up for you even when you are not around, and that can be a hard thing to do," she added.

"Sometimes it is hard to know except over time," Carol continued. "But never doubt that God will help guide us if we pray about it. We want to pray with you about that. It's always important to ask God to lead us to the right people."

"What do you think?" she asked with a confident look into Ron's eyes.

"I think you said it pretty well. They will not stop being your friend just because you're in a slump, especially when you've been solid friends for a while.

"Katie, for your good, and because we love you so much, we're gonna continue to ask you about your friends. And we'll pray – along with you – that you will always find good ones who will have a positive influence on you," Ron added. "So, if this is what it takes to be a good friend, next time we will talk about what kind of friend we should be."

CHAPTER 15

BEING A GOOD FRIEND

After praying, "Dear God, thank you for this food. Help us to use the energy we get from it to do your will. In Jesus name I pray, Amen."

Ron passed the French fries and said, "OK, tonight let's talk about what kind of friend we should be. Alex, what do you think?"

Chomping on a mouthful of hamburger, Alex swallowed, gulped some water, and spoke up, "I shouldn't get my feelings hurt too easy. I should share and be nice. I should also take up for someone if they're being picked on or bullied."

"All good answers, Alex." Ron picked up his burger to take a bite. "What about you, Katie?"

"Isn't there a scripture that says a friend loves at all times? That's kind of hard to do when a friend is being a jerk," Katie blurted out.

"Yes, it IS hard," Carol added. "But we can just stay away for a little while if we can't be nice, because a friend isn't treating us right. And I know that's a good time to pray for our friend, and for ourselves to be a good friend. Maybe it's a good time to ask them if something is wrong. How they act, and what they say and do might not really have anything to do with us."

"What else, Katie?" Ron prodded.

A little head scratching and she added, "Well, I think I am s'posed to encourage my friend, find something to compliment, but be honest about it. Be proud of 'em, not jealous, when they do well or win something. Oh, and I guess if my friend says, 'Sorry' I should forgive her."

"More excellent answers, and I can see that you're thinking hard," Ron beamed at the kids. "Now, what about you, Mom?"

"Well, they have covered a lot of good things, important things. Let me think for a minute."

Carol munched on her salad and burger. "I guess I like to figure out what my friends are good at and then work together on a project, with each using our talents to have some fun and get things done at the same time.

"Also, if they are sick or need something, it is important for me to make the time and effort to help a friend out however I can. I'm so thankful when a friend comes to my aid.

"Like when the neighbors brought us a meal when little Jack was born. That was so helpful and so nice. I know you all liked that supper, too. It wasn't just me. That is the type of friend I also want to be. Now, Dad, what about you?"

"Well, I think it is important not to talk about or gossip about our friends. If I hear something, I want to go to them and give them a chance to defend themselves. I like to take up for a friend if I hear someone saying something that's not true. I sure appreciate it when someone takes up for me.

"Or if they tell me something in confidence and say 'just between you and me,' I consider it my honor and duty – my privilege – to keep it confidential so they know they can trust me with what's on their heart," Ron said.

"Also, I should love a friend enough to speak up, in a kind and caring way when I know, in my heart, that they are wrong about something. A true and loyal friend will say something, and be honest.

"And here's another hard part: Maybe ask some questions to get your friend thinking about what they're doing or about to do. Back and forth sometimes, we should be able to talk and disagree and still be friends.

"I know I just like to be pleasant to be around. And also, I like to help others not worry or be negative. For me, and for you all too, it is important to see that a glass, like this one, is half full, not half empty. That you can decide how you view the situation. You're 'bout as happy as you decide to be each day.

"I like to have fun with my friends and help them forget their troubles or stresses for a little while, like when I play golf with my buddies. My dad used to say that if I hung out with someone who wasn't a Christian, it was my job to make sure they did not pull me down.

"It is my job to take the high road around friends who aren't Christians and at some point, show them by caring about them, tell them, lead them, help them learn how to become a Christian."

Carol added, "In Philippians. 2:3-4 (NIV) it says that as a good friend we respect our friends. *'Do nothing out of selfish ambition or vain conceit. Rather, in humility, value others above yourselves, not looking to your own interests, but each of you to the interests of the others.'*"

"Another version says, *'Do not merely look out for your own personal interests, but also for the interests of others.'*"

Carol looked up from her Bible as she heard, *"Be Ye Kind One to Another and A friend loves at all times, and a brother is born for adversity,"* Katie teased.

"Good one! That's from Proverbs 17:17. My brother and I used to tease each other back and forth with that one as well," Ron quipped.

CHAPTER 16
A STRONG FAMILY

After the family said, *"Come Lord Jesus be our Guest; And let this food to us be blest, Amen,"* it was family-talk time again. Nice habit, kinda like the old days around the kitchen table.

"Tonight, let's talk about what it takes to be a strong family and what each of us should be like in order to be a contributing family member," Ron started off the discussion at dinner. "Speak up and tell Mom and me your ideas."

"Well, remember when you told us about how you went to fire school and a fellow fire fighter told you it was going to be hard and they would yell at you like a coach, but that meant they thought you could do better, and just don't give up," Katie volunteered in a long, strung-out, excited contribution.

"Yes, ya' know it is amazing what you can accomplish if you just don't give up. I can't tell you how many times in football, I didn't think I could do one more push-up or sit-up or even run ONE. MORE. STEP. But on the other hand, I was determined that I wouldn't, I couldn't let my team down, so I just kept going.

"And at fire school," Ron continued, "that's how I climbed a 7-story ladder truck. I just kept putting one foot in front of the other. Just like they instructed, I didn't look, didn't even glance at the ground way down below. Also, I repelled down the wall out of a 4-story building. That's something I had never done before.

"That was a great beginning topic, Katie. Anything else?" Ron asked.

"Well, I guess we should just take care of our bodies like our coach teaches us, cut back on sugar and sodas and stuff, get plenty of sleep. Eat fruits and veggies, don't smoke or drink. Exercise every day. Stuff like that." Katie added. "Is that why you will only buy groceries that have nutrition, Mom? Is that why we had to prove that Ramen-type noodles actually do have a little protein before you would even buy them?"

"Yep, it is!" smiling Mom replied, "and because it's a waste of money to buy things that don't have any food value. That food doesn't do anything for your growing body. Since your Daddy and I are grown, we sure don't need the empty calories – the useless 'expanders' is what I call them!" Carol eyed Ron with a mutual smirky smile. "It doesn't make us stronger. Those foods probably make us weaker and get old faster!"

"What about you, Mom?" Alex asked.

"Hmmm. Well, I think nowadays we overlook the importance, the satisfaction, of a job well done. If we just give our kids things over and over, that you didn't do anything to really earn it, Dad and Mom made you miss out on a sense of accomplishment. There's pride in doing a good job yourself.

"My interpretation of Colossians 3:23 says, *'Whatever you do, work at it with all your heart, as working for the Lord, not for men.'* And besides that, we all need to remember what a good work ethic is, like Grandma and Grandpa's generation had."

"So that's why you won't just do things for us?" Katie quipped.

"Exactly. You got that concept down, smart girl!" Mom smiled.

"It's the same if the government just gives people things instead of training people and helping them to get jobs so that they can be proud of what they contribute to make things better for themselves and everybody else," Dad added.

"You probably haven't heard it, but there's an old saying, 'If you give a man a fish, you feed him for a day. If you teach a man to fish, you feed him for a lifetime.'

"That's what we're talking about here!

"Yes, that's also why we only buy what you need. You can earn money and save up to buy things you want, but we expect you to tithe first," Ron finished up. "You still remember what tithing means, right?"

"Yep, that means we need to give at least 1/10th of our money back to God, because it came from Him," Alex responded while also grinning as Dad beamed at him.

"What else, Alex? What do you think makes our family strong?" Carol asked.

"Well, you both taught us to be honest, and to pray, and to obey you and God. Don't those things make us strong and make our family stronger?" he asked.

"Absolutely," Ron replied, "and I want to add that I hope we, as your mom and dad, are teaching you self-motivation. That means when you find things that need to be done, you do it yourself instead of ignoring it or waiting to be told what to do.

"Perfect example: Like the other day when Katie noticed Alex had on a dirty shirt and helped him change it before we went to Wednesday night church.

"And for somebody like me that works hard at the fire department, self-motivation helps the boss to notice you and your attention to details. It will give you an edge to get raises and promotions, well unless you ARE the boss! Then you will notice workers that are self-motivated!

"Something else here, too. I think we are a respectful family," Dad added. "We honor each other for the most part, and we are respectful of other people, like our friends. People appreciate that. We are hardworking. If we don't have the money for something, we figure out a way to do it ourselves, which is often better quality than if we'd bought it, anyway!

"We also 'go the extra mile.' That's actually in the Bible. Let me find it. Here it is. Matthew 5:41 (NIV) says, *'If anyone forces you to go one mile, go with them two miles.'* And verse 40 says, *'If anyone wants to sue you and take your shirt, give them your coat as well.'*

"We surely all know that's not easy, but it is important to always do our best, even when no one is watching.

"You, Katie.

"You, Alex.

"You, little Jack.

"You, Mom.

"And me too!

"All right, now – who wants to have game night after we get the dishes done?"

"I do. I do!" Katie and Alex chimed in.

Carol went to put little Jack to bed, singing "Jesus Loves Me" over and over as she nursed him so the family could have an evening of fun together.

"Jesus loves me, this I know. For the Bible tells me so. Little ones to Him belong. They are weak, but He is strong. Yes, Jesus loves me. Yes, Jesus loves me. Yes, Jesus loves me, the Bible tells me so."

CHAPTER 17

TEACH OUR CHILDREN TO GUARD AGAINST DECEPTION

"Katie, we had your grandparents pick up the boys so we can spend some time with you," Carol said as she sat down on the bed. "We'd like for you to come down so we can talk."

Finally, Katie pulled herself off of her bed and made her way to the kitchen. Ron was already sitting at the table, eating toast and drinking his coffee.

Carol began, "Katie, awhile back you mentioned that you wish you were a boy. And I think you said you think trans is cool. Is that right?"

"W-well, that's what some of the other kids say," Katie stuttered.

"OK, but what do you yourself think, Katie?" Ron asked.

"Well, it's the fad these days."

"Does that mean you should do it?" Carol looked at Katie straight in, eye to eye.

"I guess not."

"Then tell us, help Mom and me understand why you are interested in this," Ron quizzed.

"Well, I guess I'm not really interested in trans so much. It just seemed kinda interesting at first."

"Well, what else is going on at school that we should or would want to know about?" Ron added.

"Well, we study SEL in homeroom," Katie glanced at her dad while filling up on her Cheerios.

"What is that? What does SEL mean?" Carol jumped in.

"Umm, lemme see. It stands for Social Emotional Learning. They say it helps us know how to act with others when we feel upset, like losing a ballgame. Some kids sit down and pout, but our coach taught us we should line up and high five the other team, win or lose. Then we figure out what we could have done better. You know, to learn from it."

"Well, that sounds like a good idea," Dad chimed in. "Anything else?"

"Yeah, it also teaches us things like who to ask when we need help. First, we try to figure it out by ourselves. Then we ask a friend. If we can't come up with an answer, we ask a teacher. Then if none of that works, we can ask our parents, and then our neighbors. It's called the Circle of Influence or something like that."

"So, they tell you not to ask your parents first?" Carol questioned.

"Yeah, I guess so," Katie squirmed.

"And what do you think of that?" Ron appeared to ask nonchalantly.

"Well, you taught me to honor my mother and father, so maybe I should ask you sooner. Isn't that right?"

"Yes, I want you to feel like you can ask us anything. Tell us anything," Mom assured.

"Also, we got you a few books we'd like you to read. "The Case for Christ" by Lee Strobel, "Children Demand a Verdict" and "The Awesome Book of Bible Answers" both by Josh McDowell, and "God's Crime Scene" by J. Warner Wallace. We are also going to read them so we can talk with you about them. Which would you like to start with?"

After looking over the books, Katie said, "God's Crime Scene!"

"That sounds great!" Then out of Mom's mouth came a happy question. "Enough discussion for now. Would you like to go get some ice cream?"

"Well, yes!" Katie replied with some attitude.

"OK, let's go to the Ice Cream Shoppe." Ron grabbed his car keys.

CHAPTER 18
SINGLE MOM

As Carol enjoyed her crisp kale and cranberry salad, she asked Penny, "Wow! We've had a busy, packed week with multiple projects going on at work. I bet it's hard sometimes to handle all of this and parent your four boys. How in the world have you managed to juggle the demands at work and be a single mom? Ron and I are just now starting to figure out some challenges of parenting with two of us working on it."

"Well," Penny hesitated. "It hasn't been easy.

"I am blessed to have my mom nearby to pick up the boys when I can't make it, or stay with them when I have a meeting or some other obligation. I'll admit, I have to be pretty strict with my guys. I think there's a verse that says, 'Let your no mean no and your yes be yes.' I can't be wishy washy, or they would run all over me.

"Another thing I figured long ago is that I am in charge. Rank-wise, the boys aren't equal to me. I'm in charge. That's why, most of the time, I just TELL them what we are going to do – with courtesy and usually with a soft voice – rather than ASK them if they want to do whatever.

"Since Ethan is a junior in high school now, even though to me he's supposed to still be in the cradle, not graduating in one year. He's also an excellent cook and loves being in the kitchen. He cooks supper twice a week. That's all he has time for with baseball.

"Troy is old enough in 8th grade to do the dishes Monday through Thursday. I'm the weekend person – I do them on Friday, Saturday, and Sunday.

"The little guys help me empty the dishwasher, clear the table, and take out the trash every day.

"We scrape our own plates and take them to the sink after a meal. Also, we each clean our own rooms and bathroom every other week, at least most of the time. Sometimes we are just too busy, but that is our goal. We all tackle the living room and any touch-ups in kitchen and mud room on Saturdays."

"Do you get any time to yourself?" Carol asked.

"A little bit, after everyone is in bed at night. Also, I started a quiet time on Sunday afternoons. That's when each of us can pursue our own interests.

"It's a structured quiet time. Rule 1 is to stay away from each other and do something quiet. That means no jabbering on the phone, no TV, no video games – so they can read books, draw, whatever interests them as long as they do it alone, it's quiet, and not on a screen.

"Rule 2 is to leave me alone for an hour and a half, which sometimes stretches into a luxurious two hours. The guys honor that pretty well, so I don't have to set a timer anymore!

"I decided a long time ago that I wasn't really interested in dating or starting another relationship. Honestly, with all the boys' activities, I don't really have time for one. With my guys' ages, it would just complicate things. I have enough to handle right now.

"If God leads me there, a relationship later in life when the boys are grown and gone may be another chapter in my book of life. Maybe someday.

"Tell me, how is Katie doing?"

"Better, I think," Carol responded. "Ron and I had a talk with her. She labeled the trans talk as a fad, and said she's not really interested after all. We have tried to ignore the negative and emphasize anything positive.

"At home we have given her more responsibility and attention, qualities which seem to be drawing her back in, helping us all to understand pre-teen and teen years, and teaching everyone the value of respect and trust.

"At night in our alone time, Ron and I are also praying together about our family and seeking guidance. I think that is making the biggest difference."

"I know it must be," Penny said. "That is the most important thing, even though I sometimes fall way short in that area. I guess we'd better get back to the office and move into speedy mode to finish up some of those projects.

CHAPTER 19

GENESIS 1 IS THE ANSWER!

"Hey, Ron, my friend Stephanie at church said that when her 5th grader brought up the transgender topic, Stephanie told her that was a Genesis 1 issue. Stephanie told her daughter that she needed to read Genesis 1. So, they sat down and read it together. Stephanie said she really emphasized that God made one man and one woman, and that there is one man and one woman in a marriage," Carol said as she and Ron were about to pray during their quiet time one evening.

"All of this makes me so nervous. I just wonder if we are raising our kids right, according to God's Word, especially in these difficult times. When you look online, this stuff is plastered all over social media. There is just so much that can go wrong nowadays!"

"Well, maybe we should pray about when would be the right time to bring that up at one of our family devotionals soon," Ron suggested. "I mean, all we can do is pray and do our best to obey what we feel like God is leading us to do. It's good you have Stephanie as a friend to kinda guide us as well."

"Yes, she said Philippians 4:6-7 would be a good verse for us to memorize. It starts with *'Be anxious for nothing'* and ends with *'let your requests be made known to God.'*

I will have to look up the rest, but I guess we can and should ask the Holy Spirit to guide us, too," Carol added. "And maybe we should also be in a regular Bible study so we are better at guiding our children."

CHAPTER 20

THE MOST IMPORTANT THING

Out on the patio around the picnic table, the weather felt so nice, with just a bit of cool breeze. The family put their hands together to pray. Ron led, "Dear God, thank you for this nice weather, and that our whole family is here together. Thank you for this good food and for providing for our needs. In Jesus name."

The family joined, "Amen!"

"Well, Alex, now that you're about to turn 6, we think it's time to tell you how to become a Christian," Carol smiled as they passed the taco fixins. "Do you know what that means?"

"Well, I've seen people baptized at church," Alex said, scratching his head and looking a bit puzzled.

"Katie, what can you tell Alex about becoming a Christian?" Ron quizzed.

Katie looked up from drizzling queso onto tortilla chips. "Well, you say a prayer asking Jesus into your heart."

Ron eyed Katie, "So you just need to say the right words?"

"Well, no, you have to mean them. Just say them from your heart."

"Anything else?" Carol asked.

"You should ask God to forgive your sins, you know, the stuff you did wrong or messed up on," Katie added.

"Good job, Katie! And if you ask, the Bible says that Jesus will forgive our sins."

Carol looked in her Bible for just the right verse. "Remember 1John 1:9?" she recalled. *"If we confess our sins, He is faithful and just to forgive us our sins and to cleanse us from all unrighteousness."*

Then, Carol sang the song that they all knew and the children chimed in.

After smiles, cheers and resumed tacos, Ron asked, "Alex, tell us, do you know what happens if you become a Christian?"

Again, Alex looked puzzled, but more comfortable on this issue.

"You go to heaven," Katie beamed, even before Alex could swallow and answer.

"Yes, Katie, that's right! It's like you're on top of a seesaw, all happy and free. But tell us this: What's the downside – what happens if you don't become a Christian?" Ron continued.

"You go to hell!" Katie said plain, solid, serious.

"W-W-What's that like?" Alex looked a little fearful.

"Well, it's always hot, really, really fire hot. And the people there would give anything for a drop of water," Katie added dramatically, and simulated a drink from her lemonade cup.

"Now Alex, for sure, your daddy and I don't want you to feel pressured to do any of this before you feel you feel like it's time, or before you're sure that Jesus is calling you to do it, but we do think you're now old enough to know about it,"

Carol paused briefly, comforted everyone with her cherished "Mom understands" smile, and scooped up some more guacamole with a tortilla chip.

CHAPTER 21
ONE-ON-ONE

"Hey, Ron! I was reading an article about spending time with each child one-on-one to give 'em the time and attention they need and to help them stay out of trouble. The article referenced the old-fashioned one-room schoolhouse, and how each child got time from the teacher, as well as from the older students.

"It was a common study hall time every day, when big kids partnered with their assigned little guys, and throughout the day if it was needed. Compared to the public schools now, with the children sorted by age, the one-on-one time from the teacher in the classroom may only be about one minute per hour at the most. And none of the older-to-younger teaming.

"Hmmm, that sounds interesting, but what are you getting at?" Ron quizzed.

"Well, the article suggested 20 minutes one-to-one, with each child each day or several times a week, whether scheduled or impromptu. The parent stops – intentionally stops – all other activity, phone and all, and just does what that child wants to do or needs help with, including homework. But the child chooses, and the parent goes along.

"I'd love to try and do that, but I don't have an extra hour each evening. Do you think you could help? If we work together, can you help with that and maybe spend 20 minutes with one or two of the kids?" Carol asked.

"Talk about one-to-one communication," Ron almost interrupted. "My mother did something like that. She would 'counsel' us at least once a week by always asking something like, 'OK, Ronnie, tell me one thing, just one thing, that was good about today.'

"It didn't take long, and I could always think of something, big or small, serious or silly," he smiled. "Then she, or my dad, would always ask the other side too. 'What went wrong today, what was hard today?'"

Ron's smiled, wrinkled forehead, along with a shrug of his shoulders, brought back nostalgia of several different emotions.

"How about if we start with three nights a week and make out a schedule, a wall chart or a wall calendar, that they can look at too, so we all know what we are each responsible for?"

"OK," Carol reached for the calendar that was always open on her desk. "What nights are best for you? I think I can commit to Mondays, Tuesdays, and Fridays."

"I think Tuesday, Wednesday, and Thursday work for me," Ron replied.

"So, I'll spend 20 minutes with Katie on Mondays," Carol wrote on her desk calendar. "What if you spend 20 minutes with Jack on Tuesdays, and I'll take Alex?"

"Sounds good," Ron nodded.

"Then on Wednesday, you can spend 20 minutes with Katie, and on Thursday you take 20 minutes with Alex. I'll spend 20 minutes with Jack on Friday. This is getting complicated," Carol mused, with her mouth skewed to the side in thought.

Ron looked over the schedule. "What if we call that good for now? That way, each child has 20 minutes with each parent once a week. If we continue our family devotional and game night on Saturdays, we are doing pretty good for now. We can always add to it later."

"That's a good idea. I'll take care of a calendar for them to look at and put a check-mark on it when we're done with whatever is going on night by night. Nothing like teaching a few simple organization skills as we go," Carol added.

"Maybe we should journal about how each child acts the day they get the one-on-one time just to see if it is making a difference.

Nothing formal, just a few observations or thoughts. We can make our notes in here in our bedroom, out of public view," Carol suggested.

"OK, it's worth a try," Ron yawned and headed to the shower to get ready for bed.

CHAPTER 22
WE'RE LEARNING A LOT!

"I can't believe how much we've learned and changed over the past few months since we started having a quiet time and praying over our children at night, and praying regularly at meals, and having the one-on-one times. I hope it makes them happy and secure," Carol said with a joyful tone as she got ready for bed.

"Good things, so many good things have come out of this."

"Like what," Ron asked while taking off his shoes and socks and rubbing his feet.

"Well, we've taken Jack off of three feedings a day. Removing one feeding at a time over several months has worked well for us," Carol smiled.

"I also like, mostly like, our dinner discussions, even though at first they were a little worrisome.

"The house is much more organized since we labeled the drawers with pictures and now have a time each night to 'zip up the house,'" Ron reflected.

"It's been uncharted waters, but Katie seems to be more a part of our family since the three of us had that talk," Carol sighed. "She's been, and I know I am, so much more pleased with our giving her lots of deserved praise and more, really recognizable responsibility."

"Yes," responded Ron. "That has made a big difference in our family. I like that we talked to Alex now that he's in kindergarten. He's still a little guy, but now he knows we're keeping up with what he's learning at school. And he will always know that we loved and cared about him enough to watch over him in this important way."

"Knowing that we want our children to feel free and safe, actually encouraged, to tell us if there is anything discussed or happening that we might not approve of or believe in based on the Scriptures is a big thing for any kid and any parent. And I love that we are doing just that!" Carol deliberately squeezed closer to Ron.

"And we've recognized we need to also be in a Bible study to keep up as parents. I know there are some Moms Bible Studies, but I'd us like to go together. Maybe the Bible Study Fellowship, which usually also has great Bible classes for kids, would work for both of us. What do you think?" Carol asked.

"That sounds wise, if we can squeeze it into our busy schedules," he responded.

"Oh! And we still need to talk about Genesis 1," she added. "I believe that is the answer for all of this gender confusion that is being promoted, even praised, all over the place!"

"We can talk about that next," Ron said with a comic, exaggerated whisk of his forehead. "For right now, we'll just pat our kids – and ourselves – on the backs and say, 'Jobs well done!'"

And they started their nightly prayer time with lots of praise.

If you need help for yourself and your children to be able to take a stand for your family's Christian values in education and in the world, contact us for a free 1-on-1 Strategy Session: edempower777@gmail.com

Education Empowerment Coach
Susan Perez

PART 2

CHAPTER 23

I'M NOT SURE WHAT TO DO AS A PARENT

If You're Thinking You Are Not Ready to Be a Parent, Here's How This Book Can Help!

Let's look at how to raise STRONG CHILDREN that are IN the world, but not OF the world. We must nurture our children in as many aspects of their lives as possible.

This means that the parents must put the child's needs before their own.

Here are some examples of how parents can help set your child up for success:

- Make sure they sleep enough. Sleep gives the body and brain time to grow and develop. Toddlers should get about 12–13 hours of sleep a day. Provide them with a quiet, peaceful place at naptime and bedtime. It might be good to use a soothing sound app or music to block out any noises that could wake them up before they are ready.

- Children should play outside for a little while each day. Fresh air, sunshine, and exercise are important for healthy development.

- Allow your child free time to be creative.

- Limit screen time to 30 minutes a day for educational, supervised videos like Blippi, Cocomelon, or Christian apps like Minno and Yippee! Even though these shows are educational, they are so full of colors, sounds, and action that nothing in the real world can compete. Some research is showing more children are nearsighted, due to screen time. So, limit exposure. Also, screen time shortens a child's attention span. Take them with you the rest of the time so they learn while they help you cook, clean, do yard work, or help in the community... or sometimes just let them play.

- Only provide children food that is nutritious. If food comes in a package, have your child show you in the Nutrition Facts on the back of the package exactly what healthful value that food contains before you agree to pay for it.
   o How much protein is there?
   o Are there vitamins?
   o How much fiber does it have? (NOTE: Sodium, sugar, and carbohydrates do not count as food value.)

   Some foods that are high in nutrition are:
   o Fresh fruits and vegetables
   o Protein such as meats, eggs, yogurt (with fewer than 20 grams of sugar), peanut butter made from ground up peanuts, cheese, etc.
   o Whole grains (whole grain cereal with less than 13 grams of sugar, rice, bread that does not have high fructose sugar which your body cannot digest)

PART 2 of this book is NOT to be read like a book. These are references and resources that are helpful for parenting.

HOW TO USE PART 2:

Twice a year before each birthday and Christmas or Fourth of July, open this book to the section that gives gift suggestions for the child's upcoming stage of development. Look at the age they will be for their next birthday.

For example, if they are turning 3, look in the section entitled 3 to 4 Years to see what each child could likely do over the upcoming year. Some gift ideas are underlined within the developmental lists. There are more gift ideas at the end of each chapter.

The organization of this book provides a general overview or brief summary of each age at the beginning of each chapter in PART 2.

Next, there are lists of developmental milestones listed under 7 categories: **1. Physical, 2. Cognitive, 3. Language, 4. Social – Emotional, 5. Self Care, 6. Spiritual, and 7. Responsibility Measures** by age.

It is common knowledge that each child is unique and develops in his own frame of time. This book describes what many children can do at each stage. Should the time frame or sequence vary, don't fret or be anxious. Therefore, a child performing these skills a little early or a little later or in a different sequence, is nothing to get excited about. Basically, these lists can be used as a guide for developmental activities as children pass through these stages.

Look at **PHYSICAL DEVELOPMENT** and **COGNITIVE DEVELOPMENT** lists to see if there are skills a child has not tried. If they haven't tried to stand on one foot by age 3, demonstrate standing or balancing on one foot and ask the child if they can also do that. Teach them. Show them. Help them learn. Be observant.

If there is concern about the child's **LANGUAGE DEVELOPMENT**, detailed lists are available by age.

SELF CARE teaches parents how to encourage a child to do things for self and practice indeoendence.

SOCIAL - EMOTIONAL section lists ways that a child can learn to get along with others.

Please NOTE: There is **SPIRITUAL DEVELOPMENT** information included for each age which gives ideas on how to help "Train up a child in the way he should go". **Indeed, this may be the most important section of this book for Raising STRONG CHILDREN!**

This section starts with two or more Scriptures for the child to memorize with the parents. Mom and/or Dad can say these Scriptures at bedtime along with singing a few songs to infants that help establish a bedtime routine, as well as shape earliest inklings of reading, listening, singing, and music.

When children know Scripture, it helps them to learn the principles for making wise decisions. There are many ways to memorize scripture.

The spiritual milestones are key in helping each child develop and retain a biblical worldview. Spiritual development is extremely important for creating a foundation for each child's beliefs and actions. These foundations last a lifetime.

RESPONSIBILITY MEASURES that are age-appropriate help parents to determine if they are doing too much FOR their child vs. teaching each child to do what he can on his own. Sometimes it may seem easier for the parent to clean up after a child, but teaching a child to do a chore or job allows that child to feel the satisfaction of a job well done. Don't deprive him of that. Remember the "teach him how to fish" folk lesson.

When a child can pick something up, he is old enough to put a toy away. This helps the family with all the chores and tidying up that need to be done every single day. It also creates a more organized and peaceful atmosphere. Working together promotes family unity. As a result, each child will learn that he is a valued part of the family. This leads to self-confidence and self-sufficiency. Talents emerge while memories are created.

Give praise for jobs completed! An example might be, "Thank you for putting your toy on the shelf where it goes! That makes this room feel more organized. Good job! And it makes me happy (that I didn't even have to) -OR- (even if I did have to) remind you."

Teaching age-appropriate responsibilities helps parents handle the challenges of parenting without feeling overwhelmed.

There are developmentally appropriate **Gift Ideas** at the end of each chapter for children about to turn that age.

The final section of each chapter has some **Parenting Tips** and stories to bring this information to life!

NOTE: Some of these topics do not begin until the child is at an appropriate age.

Let's get started.

CHAPTER 24
AN INFANT IS SO FLOPPY! CAN I DO THIS?

BIRTH TO 3 MONTHS

Newborns are helpless and must depend on parents and caregivers to notice what they need and help them grow into healthy, well-adjusted children. This requires parents giving up what they might want to do or where they might choose to go, often putting the child's interests and needs above their own.

Parenting is one of the most challenging AND most rewarding adventures you will ever be a part of. Children can bring the biggest challenges and rewards! The days are LONG, but the years fly by, so enjoy all the special moments. They don't last long.

Let's look at what newborns typically know. Knowing and noticing these things will help a parent to be more attentive and relaxed.

Newborns begin the sucking, rooting (explained in the lists below), and grasping reflexes. Infants typically tug and pull on their own hands, clench them into fists, and bring them to their mouths.

Head control comes from an infant holding her head up for a few seconds, especially when lying on her stomach. Tummy Time helps to develop strength in the baby's neck, back, and even arms. She can focus on objects and faces that are moving. She detects different voice pitch and volume.

It is important to read/sing to newborns, or even to the baby in the womb. She may not understand the words yet, but she will learn to associate books and songs with love and affection.

GIFT IDEAS

NOTE: GIFT IDEAS are at the end of each chapter.
Also, NOTE the gift ideas underlined and boldfaced items in developmental lists.

PHYSICAL - GROSS MOTOR

Newborn

- Reflex behaviors - head thrown back, arms apart, legs extended, then arms brought back or head turned to side, arms on that side extended, other arm flexed
- Suspended prone – head, hands completely down
- Prone – rotates head to either side, hips raised, knees drawn up

1 Month

- Pulled to sit – complete head lag
- On stomach – lifts head and holds
- Held sitting – head forward, back rounded, head lifted briefly
- Prone – makes alternating crawling movements
- Straightens leg when bottom of foot is pressed
- Lifts head when held at caretaker's shoulder
- On back – head to one side with same side are straight and leg straight, opposite arm bent and leg bent (asymmetrical tonic neck reflex)
- Turns head to side

2 Months

- Thrusts arm and legs in play
- On stomach – chin sometimes lifted off bed
- Lying on back flexes and extends legs, lifting them an inch or two
- Turns from side to back
- Held sitting or standing, head position predominantly sags

- Suspended face down – head held level with body briefly lifted above
- On stomach – holds head up well off mat
- Legs kick in sequence

3 Months

- Suspended face down, head held above level of body
- On stomach – hips lowered, knees bent
- Prone – rests on forearm, raising head and chest
- Held standing – lifts foot
- Attempts to roll from stomach to side

FINE MOTOR

Newborn

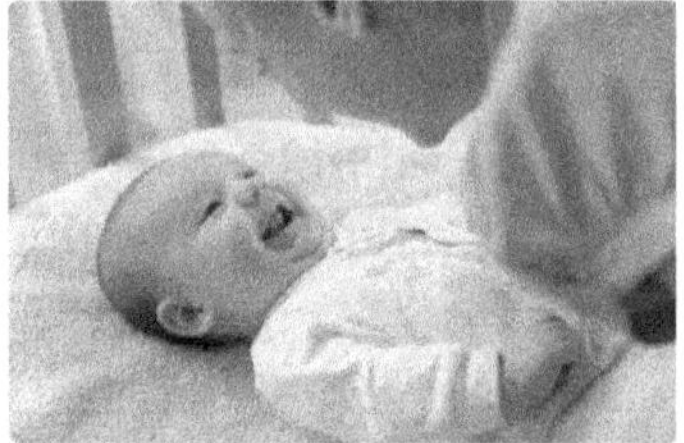

- Fisted hands rest near face
- Grasp reflex – clench small object on contact
- Regards colorful object momentarily

2 Months

- Holds hands together
- Holds rattle 5 to10 seconds before dropping
- Grasp reflex disappearing
- Moves arms symmetrically
- Regards colorful object for a few seconds
- Lying on back – follows moving person with eyes
- Looks at object or person for prolonged period

3 Months

- Reaches for object with both hands, often misses
- Fingers loosely closed
- Explores objects such as rattle placed in both hands
- Tracks object with eyes from side to side he is facing to midline

- Brings hands to midline - lying on back
- Activates arms on sight of toy
- Blinks at sudden visual stimulus
- Follows with eyes past midline
- Follows with eyes downward
- Thumbs no longer held in hand
- Looks from one object to another
- Grasps objects placed in both hands
- Grasp and traction reflex – resists toy being pulled away
- COGNITIVE

COGNITIVE

Newborn

- Responds to sound of bell or **rattle**

1 Month

- Responds to voice
- Cry differs to express specific discomfort (hunger, wet, cold, etc.)
- Quiets when picked up
- Shows pleasure when touched or handled
- Responds to sounds

2 Months

- Visually recognizes parent
- Social smile in response to stimulation
- Responds to voice
- Inspects surroundings

3 Months

- Looks at face and eyes of person talking to him
- Babbles, coos when talked to
- Looks longer at human face than at objects
- Chuckles
- Looks more at surroundings in a new place

- Vocalizes emotional state (anger and pleasure)
- Smiles at sound of familiar voice
- Quietens at a sound heard out of sight
- Searches with eyes for sound (side to side only)
- Anticipates breast or bottle with excitement
- Alternates glance between 2 visual targets
- Follows visually at point where slowly moving object disappears

LANGUAGE

Newborn

- Cry is monotonous, nasal, one breath long – reflexive vocalization
- Cries when hungry or uncomfortable

1 Month

- Quiets or startles to sound of a rattle or a bell
- Makes small throaty noises
- Responds to voice
- Makes comfort sounds – reflexive vocal ("k," "m," "aaah," or "nnn")
- Makes sucking sounds
- Cry varies in pitch, length, and volume to indicate needs such as hunger, pain

2 Months

- Makes single vowel sounds
- Anticipatory excitement
- Smiling "rrr" sounds – vocal babbling in "a" and "e" group
- Cry stronger and discriminating
- Searches with eyes for sound

3 Months

- Babbles or coos when talked to
- Looks at face and eyes of person talking to him

- Disassociates vocalizations from bodily movement – vocalizes when lying still
- Cries more rhythmically with mouth opening and closing
- Squeals
- Cries mainly when hungry
- Beginning to form consonant sounds
- Quietens at a sound heard out of sight

SELF CARE

Newborn

- Demonstrates sucking reflex
- Demonstrates rooting reflex – turns head to locate source of food when cheek is touched
- Opens and closes mouth in response to food stimulus

1 Month

- Coordinates sucking, swallowing and breathing
- Sleeps nights 4 to 8 hour intervals
- Stays awake for longer periods without crying – usually in PM
- Naps frequently

2 Months

- Suck and swallow reflex becomes more voluntary than reflex
- Brings hand to mouth
- Brings hand to mouth with toy or object

3 Months

- Recognizes bottle visually

SOCIAL - EMOTIONAL

Newborn

- Enjoys and needs a great deal of physical contact and tactile stimulation
- Regards face

- Molds and relaxes body when held, cuddles
- Draws attention to self when in distress

1 Month

- Establishes eye contact

2 Months

- The feeding posture, which involves holding the child with her face directed toward the person holding her, enhances interpersonal relationships
- Smiles reflexively, typically directed toward caretaker
- Needs security caretaker provides for development of self-realization

3 Months

- Responds with smile when socially approached
- Stops unexplained crying

SPIRITUAL

Each **SPIRITUAL SECTION** starts with 2 Scriptures to say aloud every night.

"Train up a child in the way he should go and when he is old, he will not depart from it." Proverbs 22:6 King James Version

"This is the day that the LORD has made. We will rejoice and be glad in it." Psalm 118:24 New American Standard Bible

- Listens to short (5 minute) bedtime Bible story and a 5 to10 word Scripture that parent is trying to memorize which helps to establish a bed-time routine
- Relaxes hearing caregiver sing a song about Jesus ("Jesus Loves Me" or "This is the Day that the LORD has Made," "He's Got the Whole World in His Hands") or hearing songs from YouTube links: https://youtu.be/2TIZ4ibzG7A
- https://youtu.be/2TIZ4ibzG7A)
- Nurses at bedtime while hearing caregiver saying a prayer for self, family, and baby

Note to Parents:

Nursing has distinct advantages. It is a time to relax and bond with your baby. Most doctors recommend nursing a baby about 15 – 20 minutes on each breast at a feeding and to feed every 3 to 4 hours. Read a story to your little one while you feed/nurse her.

At the bedtime feeding, read a short (5 minutes) Bible story and say a short scripture (See Parent Cue app) to establish a bedtime routine for you and your baby. Also, sing a song like "Jesus Loves Me." You don't have to have a magnificent voice for your child to be comforted by the rhythm of your song and cadence of the words.

Jesus Loves Me Lyrics
Jesus loves me! This I know,
For the Bible tells me so;
Little ones to Him belong;
They are weak, but He is strong.

Refrain:

Yes, Jesus loves me!
Yes, Jesus loves me!
Yes, Jesus loves me!
The Bible tells me so.

Jesus loves me! This I know,
As He loved so long ago,
Taking children on His knee,
Saying, "Let them come to Me." **Refrain**

Jesus loves me still today,
Walking with me on my way,
Wanting as a friend to give
Light and love to all who live.
Refrain

Jesus loves me! He who died
Heaven's gate to open wide;
He will wash away my sin,
Let His little child come in.
Refrain

Jesus loves me! He will stay
Close beside me all the way;
Thou hast bled and died for me,
I will henceforth live for Thee.
Refrain

A mother or father singing this to your child is priceless.

Also, it is important for new moms to sleep when the baby sleeps. Mom needs to take naps with the baby at least during the first 3 months because of the interruptions to sleep during the night. Also, these naps will help your body to heal and recover from the ordeal of giving birth!

Related Stories:

When my son was born (my third child) I could not satisfy him with my breast milk. I fed him many times during the first few days and nights (much more often than the normal every three to four hours), but he always seemed hungry.

My neighbor said she had that problem with her boys and had to change to formula. I was hesitant to give up. I knew breast milk gave the baby immunity and was much healthier than formula. Also, it's free, and we were on a very limited income back then. In a lot of ways, breast feeding is easier, no bottles to wash, no nipples and other bottle parts to sterilize.

Any time, and with no prep needed, I could joyfully sit down and relax with my baby in my arms and let him eat. I tried something a little different. I fed him 15 minutes on each breast. Then I made a bottle of formula and let him feed until he was full and fell asleep. That was the first night we both got some sleep. After a few days of doing this, it only took breast milk to satisfy his hunger. He no longer needed the additional formula to satisfy him.

Parenting Tip: I noticed when Princess Diana was in public one time with infant Prince William, he was fussy, possibly hungry. She curled up her little finger and stuck the middle knuckle into his mouth. He sucked on it until the formal event was over. I used this trick many times after that to satisfy one of my babies until I could go to a discreet place to feed them.

GIFT IDEAS:

NOTE the <u>underlined</u> and <u>boldfaced</u> items in developmental lists. There are additional gift ideas in the **GIFT IDEAS** section at the end of each chapter.

Primerica Financial Services (and possibly other similar companies) offers a college funding plan called Sprynt where the family can make an initial investment of $250. Then the link similar to a social media page can be sent to relatives and friends, so that they can contribute to the education fund as a part of birthday or

Christmas gifts. This company has a chart that shows how much faster this builds a college nest egg than if only the parents contribute regularly. Also, the child doesn't end up with a room full of toys each holiday that may only interest him for a short time.

CHAPTER 25
SHOULDN'T MY BABY ROLL OVER BY NOW?

3 TO 6 MONTHS

At this age, most infants move more and begin to notice the world around them. They learn to roll over, sit up with support, pull their bodies forward, and pull themselves by grasping something. They put objects into their mouths, reach for objects, and play with toys. They recognize familiar faces, respond to the facial expressions of others, and imitate them.

GIFT IDEAS

*NOTE: GIFT IDEAS are at the end of each chapter. **Also, NOTE the gift ideas <u>underlined</u> <u>and</u> <u>boldfaced</u> items in developmental lists below.***

PHYSICAL - GROSS MOTOR

4 Months

- On back – head facing forward, not turned
- Pulled to sit, no head lag
- Rolls from back to side
- Suspended face down – holds head up
- Puts weight on abdomen with arms and legs straightened
- Sits propped, head steady, back curved only slightly
- Takes weight on feet briefly with underarm support

5 Months

- Holds head and chest up on forearms for long periods
- On stomach – props on hands with arm straight
- No head wobble when body is swayed
- Lifts head when lying on back
- Sits supported with back straight
- Grasps objects while sitting

6 Months

- Rolls from stomach to back
- Rolls from back to stomach
- Prone – pushes up on hands with chest and abdomen off mat
- Sits supported in **highchair**
- Bears almost all weight while standing supported and bounces
- Lifts legs high and holds them out straight when lying on back
- Grasps feet with hands when lying on back
- Protective extension of arms and legs downward when held in suspension facing the floor
- Demonstrates balance reactions when tilted while lying on stomach or back
- Rocks on abdomen
- Moves head actively in supported sitting position
- Holds head erect when leaning forward
- Assists when pulled to sitting with no head lag

PHYSICAL - FINE MOTOR

4 Months

- Grasps toy actively
- Watches movement of own hands
- Hands are usually open
- Shakes and plays with **rattle** for several minutes

- Opens hands, plays with fingers, puts hands in mouth
- Reaches toward objects, sometimes hits them
- At play, pulls covers or clothing over face
- Recovers rattle dropped on chest
- Retains dangling ring
- Follows with eyes, moving object in supported sitting position
- Turns head to follow objects

5 Months

- Picks up **cube(s)**
- Holds first cube, notices second cube
- Picks up **spoon**
- Follows with eyes – 180 degrees
- Transfers object from hand to mouth
- Uses ulnar palmer grasp – grasps object with ring finger and little finger against palm
- Uses one hand to reach for object
- Regards tiny object
- Uses palmar grasp-grasps object against palm without use of thumb

6 Months

- Rakes up raisins (or pellets) with fingers against palm
- Lifts cup by handle
- Reaches persistently
- Bangs object on table
- Follows with eyes without head movement
- Uses radial palmar grasp – grasps with thumb, index and middle fingers and palm
- Looks at distant objects
- Recovers object dropped if within easy reach
- Retains small object in each hand

<u>**COGNITIVE**</u>

4 Months

- Disturbed by angry voice
- Eyes follow dangling ring moved in arc
- Vocalizes instead of cries when alone
- Turns head toward source of voice
- Vocalizes, smiles, and reaches for familiar person
- Looks at and reaches for toy
- Turns head to sound of rattle
- Recovers rattle dropped on chest
- Enjoys repeating newly learned activity
- Uses hands and mouth for sensory exploration of objects
- Turns eyes and head to sound of hidden voice
- Plays with own hands, feet, fingers, and toes

5 Months

- Laughs aloud when lightly tickled and talked to
- Turns head to look for dropped object
- Vocalizes 3 emotional states
- Directs sounds and gestures toward objects
- Awakens or quiets to mother's voice
- Continues a familiar activity by initiating movements involved
- Holds first cube, notices second cube

6 Months

- Discriminates strangers
- Smiles and vocalizes to mirror image
- Resists attempt to take away toy
- Holds arms out to be picked up
- Drops toy and looks for it
- Vocalizes, waves limbs on hearing steps or voice
- Mouths toys
- Looks at objects while handling them
- Raises arms to be lifted

- Searches for partially hidden object
- Refuses food when full

LANGUAGE

4 Months

- Turns head toward source of voice
- Vocalizes instead of cries
- Laughs aloud in social play
- Turns head to sound of rattle
- Coos open vowels (aah), closed vowels (ee), diphthongs (oy as in boy)
- More differentiation of facial expressions
- Voice more opening and closing of oral cavity, lip movements, and lip play - "m" and "b"
- Blow-frictive sounds – "f"
- Makes sleepy sounds

5 Months

- Squeals
- Clearly recognized qualities and variations in crying
- Variety in pitch, variation, and sound formation

6 Months

- Smiles and vocalizes to mirror image
- Babbles consonant chains "ba-ba"
- Vocalizes attitudes other than crying – joy, displeasure
- Reacts to music by cooing
- Babbling with more differentiation and using syllables with "p" and "g"
- Upright position produces more sounds in front with lips and tongue tip

<u>**SELF CARE**</u>

4 Months

- Rooting reflex begins to disappear
- Pats bottle periodically while it's held for him during feeding
- Sleeps nights 10 to12 hours with night awakening
- Naps 2 or 3 times each day, about 1-4 hours
- Places both hands on bottle

6 Months

- Lifts <u>**cup with handles**</u>
- Eats strained or pureed foods

<u>**SOCIAL - EMOTIONAL**</u>

4 Months

- Vocalizes in response to adult talk and smile
- Discriminates strangers
- Socializes with strangers/anyone
- Vocalizes attitudes – pleasure and displeasure
- Shows attachment to caretaker because she has been paired with pleasant events and relief of distress

5 Months

- Becomes aware of strange situations
- Enjoys social play
- Makes approach movements to mirror
- Smiles spontaneously

6 Months

- Demands social attention
- Lifts arms to mother

<u>**RESPONSIBILITY MEASURES**</u>

Mean what you say, and your child will learn to respect that. *"But let your 'Yes' be 'Yes' and your 'No' be 'No'!"* Matthew 5:37 World English Bible

<u>**SPIRITUAL**</u>

Each Spiritual Section starts with 2 Scriptures to say aloud every night.

"Love never ends." 1 Corin 13:8 (NASB)

"Be strong in the LORD and in His mighty power." Ephesians 6:10 New Living Translation

- Listens to a short (5 minute) Bible story
- Makes eye contact with caregiver as short scripture is stated (See scripture above or Parent Cue or other similar app)
- Turns head to source of voice as song, such as "Jesus Loves the Little Children," is sung
- Attends family church regularly to establish routines, Christian friendships, and activities

Parents, you are doing Kingdom work.
Read the Bible. Sing worship songs.
Pray with your kids. Memorize Bible verses together.
Bless your children each day.
Point them to Christ with every opportunity.
Be intentional about parenting.
You are their first and best teacher.
You have a divine responsibility to introduce each child to Jesus Christ.

Note to Parents:

Continue to walk daily as when pregnant. This is healthy for you and your baby (in a stroller) to be in the fresh air and sunlight getting exercise, and listening to nature sounds. During the walk, point out things from nature that God made like the blue sky and green grass.

Maybe pick up a leaf and put it on the baby's skin while talking about "rough" and green. Continue to build vocabulary and show what all God made in the infinite variety of nature.

Suggested Activities:

Sing songs like "Baa Baa Black Sheep", "He's Got the Whole World in His Hands", "The B-I-B-L-E, That's the Book for Me"

Do Finger Plays the baby can join like Pat a Cake, Itsy Bitsy Spider, Open Them Shut Them, etc.

Play Peek-a-Boo

Ride 'em Pony bouncing on leg

Take toddler to church to begin socialization with other children and exposure to Christian activities.

Parenting Tips:

I used a small pillow that had straps with Velcro to attach it to the arm rest of the rocking chair. It cushioned my arm from the baby's head as I nursed her. This became more important as the baby got older and her head got heavier, since I nursed each baby for about 18 months. I started giving up one feeding at a time.

Starting at about 12 months, I gave up the noon feeding first since I was at work. That way, I no longer had to rush to the day care during my lunch hour or pump milk in the restroom during that time. My breast milk adjusted as the demand lessened. Later, I eliminated the 5 p.m. bottle feeding as the baby started eating table food instead. The last feeding I gave up was the one at bedtime since that was a precious bonding time and comforted the baby as she fell asleep.

Related Story:

Since I traveled for work as an education curriculum consultant or school administrator, I had a leather, hard-sided brief case that went practically everywhere with me. It looked very professional, but contained a gel ice pack (frozen to keep the breast milk cold), breast pump, bottle with the plastic liner, nipple, and lid.

I had to wear pads in my nursing bra so any leaks would not be visible. I had extra pads in the briefcase just in case I needed them. At noonish, I would take the briefcase into the stall of whatever restroom I was near and pump the milk out of each breast. I poured it into the bottle and sealed it with a nipple and lid. As soon as I got home, I took the plastic liner out of the bottle, fastened the top with a twisty-tie, and put the milk in the freezer for future use.

By the time our second child arrived, we decided mostly breast milk and some formula was a good enough combination! When I was not around, we used formula.

GIFT IDEAS:

NOTE the <u>underlined</u> <u>and</u> <u>boldfaced</u> items in developmental lists. There are additional gift ideas in the GIFT IDEAS section at the end of the chapter.

- Rattle
- Rubbery ring to hold and to chew on
- Soft cube to hold
- Toy mirror (not breakable)
- Thin blanket or cloth for peek-a-boo
- Sippy Cup
- Rubbery divided plate
- Rubbery bowls with suction on bottom
- Child's plastic ware
- Snack cup with handles and slits in lid for child to retrieve cheerios, yogurt bites, etc.)
- Small pillow to cushion care givers arm while nursing or giving a bottle

CHAPTER 26

HE'S CRAWLING!

6 TO 9 MONTHS

A child begins to grasp and pull objects toward his body, sit without support, and transfer objects from one hand to the other. He may also crawl! He can transfer an object from one hand to the other.

GIFT IDEAS

*NOTE: GIFT IDEAS are listed at the end of each chapter. **Also, NOTE the gift ideas <u>underlined</u> <u>and</u> <u>boldfaced</u> items in developmental lists below.***

<u>PHYSICAL - GROSS MOTOR</u>

7 Months

- On stomach – bears weight on one hand
- Sits briefly without support
- Bounces when held standing
- Pushes up on hands and knees and rocks

8 Months

- Changing from stomach to sitting and sitting to stomach using the sides of crib or pen for support
- Balances well when sitting hands free
- Crawls backward on abdomen by pushing with arms

- Crawls on belly – arms used simultaneously to pull body forward
- Crawls bilaterally on belly – alternating one side of body at a time
- Pulls self to stand using chair or other object for support

9 Months

- Sits steadily on floor for 10 minutes
- Protective extension reflex – extends arms when toppled from sitting position (front and side)

PHYSICAL - FINE MOTOR

7 Months

- Plays with paper when it is offered
- Holds one **cube** and takes another
- Pulls out **large peg from peg board**
- Grasps and transfers **ring** from hand to hand

8 Months

- Shakes **bell**
- Manipulates toy actively with wrist movements
- Reaches and grasps object with elbow extended
- Uses radial digital grasp – using thumb, index and middle fingers without use of palm
- Rakes tiny object
- Flings toys awkwardly

9 Months

- Lines up cube in one hand with one in other hand
- Holds, bites and chews cracker or cookie
- Grasps with thumb and forefinger

<u>**COGNITIVE**</u>

7 Months

- Pats mirror image
- Bangs and shakes toys
- Plays with paper
- Touches toy or adult's hand to restart an activity
- Reaches for second object purposefully
- Works for desired out-of-reach object
- Distinguishes between friendly and angry voices
- Shows interest in sounds of objects
- Responds to facial expressions
- Retains 2 of 3 objects offered

8 Months

- Holds one cube and takes another
- Repeat actions that produce a noise
- Plays peek-a-boo
- Follows trajectory of moving object
- Looks for family members or pets when named

9 Months

- Shakes head no-no
- Imitates sounds
- Responds to name with head turn, eye contact, smile
- Stops activity at disapproving vocal tones
- Responds consistently to own name
- Differentiates family from strangers
- Plays 2 to 3 minutes with single toy
- Slides toy or object on surface
- Responds to simple requests with gestures

LANGUAGE

7 Months

- Combines vowel sounds "oo"
- Looks and vocalizes to own name
- Babbles to people
- Hearing is improving, talking in higher pitches to include full range
- Imitation beginning
- Whispers
- Plays with sounds on both inhalation and exhalation

8 Months

- Combines syllables "da-da," "ba-ba," and "ma-ma"
- Shouts for attention
- Understands and uses gestures in more advanced manner than spoken language
- Listens selectively to familiar words
- Turns to voice

9 Months

- Shakes head no-no
- Responds to name with head turn, eye contact, smile
- Imitates playful sounds
- Waves or responds to bye-byes
- Vocalizes exclamations
- Important stage - discriminates mother from others
- Attends to simple command
- More exact about imitations
- Uses double syllables – "mama", "dada"

SUGGESTED BOOKS TO READ – *The Wheels on the Bus, The Very Hungry Caterpillar* by Eric Carle, *Freight Train* by Donald Crews

<u>**SELF CARE**</u>

7 Months

- Uses tongue to move food in mouth

8 Months

- Finger feeds dry cereal, bits of meat, vegetables
- Bites, chews toys during play
- Mouths and gums small pieces of soft food
- Bites food voluntarily
- Bites and chews toys

9 Months

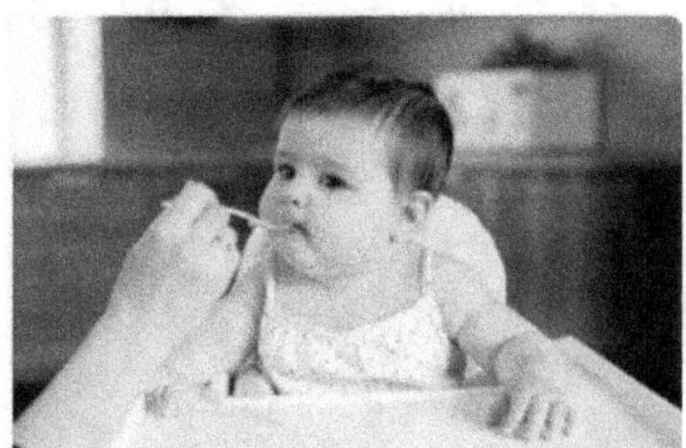

- Holds bites and chews cracker and cookie
- Holds own bottle
- Begins to hold spoon
- Remains dry one hour at a time
- Demonstrates adaptive movements during dressing or undressing

<u>**SOCIAL - EMOTIONAL**</u>

7 Months

- Enjoys frolic play (4 to 8 months)
- Repeats enjoyable activities
- Explores adult features
- Smiles at mirror image

8 Month

- Recognizes mother visually

9 Months

- Displays stranger anxiety
- Distinguishes self as separate from mother
- Shows anxiety over separation from mother
- Responds playfully to mirror

RESPONSIBILITY MEASURES

- Allows parent to wipe gums with a clean cloth 2 times a day before he gets any teeth
- Cooperates as parent starts cleaning every surface of each tooth 2 times a day as soon as they come in
- Eats only healthy, low-sugar foods and drinks
- Begins first dental visits and develops a happy attitude about visiting the dentist

SPIRITUAL

Each Spiritual Section starts with 2 Scriptures to say aloud every night.

"Praise the LORD!" Psalm 106:1 (NASB)

"With my mouth I will give thanks abundantly to the LORD." Psalm 109:30a (NASB) (Use a picture or motion to act this verse out.)

- Listens to a short (5 minute) **Bible story**
- Makes eye contact with caregiver as short scripture is stated (See scriptures above or Parent Cue or other similar app)
- Turns head to source of voice as song, such as "Jesus Loves the Little Children" and/or "Hallelujah Praise Ye the LORD!" is sung
- Attends family church regularly to establish routine, Christian friendships and activities

CHAPTER 27
SHE'S WALKING! SHE TOOK SOME STEPS!!

9 TO 12 MONTHS

Many babies can pull themselves into a seated position, stand, and even take a few steps. A child can pick up and throw objects, roll a ball, and grasp objects with the thumb and finger(s).

Additional fine motor skills also develop. She can look at pictures in a book and stop when told "no-no". She can finger feed most foods, and many children finally start to sleep through the night.

GIFT IDEAS:

NOTE the <u>underlined</u> <u>and</u> <u>boldfaced</u> items in developmental lists below.

There are additional gift ideas in the **GIFT IDEAS** section at the end of the chapter.

PHYSICAL - GROSS MOTOR

10 Months

- Lowers self to sitting, holding onto a rail
- Crawls on hands and knees
- Reciprocally - alternating arm and leg of opposite sides; stomach up
- Bilaterally – alternating one side of body at a time; stomach up
- Stands with one hand held
- Sits from standing without holding on

11 Months

- Side steps holding onto furniture
- Extends arms to rear when toppled from sitting position
- Walks with one or both hands held
- Twists around to pick up object while sitting
- Standing, may pivot body 90 degrees
- Stands alone, momentarily
- Extends head, back, hips, and legs when held round the trunk in mid-air suspension

12 Months

- Standing alone, takes 2 or 3 steps without support
- Creeping rapidly on hands and knees
- Walks – takes 5 steps without falling
- Bear walking – creeps on hands and feet
- Lifts one foot off floor while standing

PHYSICAL - FINE MOTOR

10 Months

- Index finger begins to point or pokes into holes or hooks and pulls
- Uncovers toy seen hidden
- Hits **cup** with **spoon**
- Manipulates cube and cup together

11 Months

- Pulls ring at the end of string
- Uses pincer type grasp to obtain cereal or pellet
- Holds crayons and makes marks
- Removes **pegs** from **peg board**
- Takes objects out of containers
- Extends wrist (9 to10 months)
- Releases object voluntarily

12 Months

- Removes lid of box to find toy he/she has seen hidden
- Beats 2 objects together
- Builds tower of 2 to 3 **blocks** after demonstration
- Places one cube in cup

COGNITIVE

10 Months

- Responds to verbal request
- Lines up cube in one hand with 1 in other hand
- Stirs with spoon in imitation
- Points, pokes, pries, touches with index finger
- Stops activity when told "no-no"
- Uncovers toy seen hidden
- Looks at pictures in book

11 Months

- Repeats performance when laughed at
- Pulls string to obtain

12 Months

- Vocalizes to music
- Imitates gesture made by adult
- Listens selectively to familiar words
- Guides action on toy manually
- Throws objects
- Drops objects systematically
- Uses locomotion to regain object and resumes play
- Listens to speech without being distracted by other sources
- Places **cylinders** in **matching hole** in **containers**
- Stacks **plastic rings**
- Moves to rhythms of **songs**

<u>**LANGUAGE**</u>

10 Months

- Responds to verbal requests
- Stops activity when told "no-no"
- Shakes head for "no"
- Reacts clearly to his name
- Says one word that expresses whole sentence
- More drooling as a result of standing and attempts at equilibrium
- Plays with sounds with greater inflection and makes funny noises – cough, click tongue, vibrate lips
- Imitates sounds made by others

12 Months

- Follows simple instructions
- Uses double syllables besides "ma-ma," and "da-da"
- Jabbers expressively – the first consonant sounds are usually bilabials "m" "b" "p" (often heard in conjunction with feeding) Also "d" and "t" may be heard at feeding time
- Language understanding increases, interest in music, reacts by moving to rhythm 
- Says first words – free speech
- Performs gesture commands - - "pick me up"
- Babbles monologue when left alone
- Repeats sounds or gestures if laughed at
- Speech may plateau as child learns to walk
- Unable to talk while walking

<u>**SELF CARE**</u>

10 Months

- Attempts to remove obstacles in efforts to find lost toy

12 Months

- Finger feeds self for part of meal
- Takes off hat, shoes
- Drinks from cup held for him
- Drools less except when teething
- Holds spoon
- Sleeps nights 12 to14 hours
- Naps once or twice each day 1 to 4 hours (may refuse morning nap)
- Cooperates with dressing by extending arm or leg

SOCIAL - EMOTIONAL

10 Months

- Cooperates in **games**

12 Months

- Struggles against lying down
- Shows like/dislike for certain people, objects, places
- Let's only mother meet his needs
- Extends toy to show others, not for release
- Tests parental reactions during feeding
- Tests parental reactions at bedtime
- Engages in simple imitative play
- Explores environment enthusiastically – safety precautions important
- Demonstrates awareness of outside world
- Communication with others by making sounds

SPIRITUAL

Each Spiritual Section starts with 2 Scriptures to say aloud every night.

"Your hands created me and fashioned me." Psalm 119:73a (NASB)

"Oh give thanks to the LORD, for He is good." Psalm 106:1b (NASB)

Since your children are going to imitate you, give them something to imitate!

- Puts hands together, close eyes, and bows head during prayer before each meal
- Begins to repeat prayer after or with parent at mealtime and bed time
- Listens and begins to sing as parent sings "Jesus is the Light," "Praise Him, Praise Him All Ye Little Children, God is Love," "Hallelujah Praise Ye the LORD!"
- Repeats short Scripture

RESPONSIBILITY MEASURES

Discuss sharing often and expect each child to share. Say "That was Jack's choice. You'll need to pick something else for now" ... if Jack had the toy first. In a few minutes, the parent can ask Jack if he is ready for some new toy and encourage him to share the toy he has. It is also important to let kids work out conflict over toys on their own.

If a child can pick up toys, he can put toys away.

Parenting Tips:

Sing songs like "The Wheels on the Bus" or "Jesus Loves Me" that have motions for baby to sing along and do the motions or sign language with a parent. Teach the child simple sign language for "please" and "thank you" for "more" and "all done". Give lavish praise for good things done. (Avoid candy or sweets for rewards as most have no food value and interfere with appetite for healthy foods. Remember sugar can be addictive.)

Try to distract (out of sight, out of mind) to help baby to mind and stay away from anything harmful.

Help your baby to develop a cheerful disposition and distract him from crying by meeting his need or giving him something else to focus on. Help make the other parent a hero. "Look how strong daddy is!" "Mommy is so smart!"

If young children throw a fit when told 'no' about something that is not good for them (like when they ask for candy right before a meal, which spoils their appetite for the good food being prepared), it is important NOT to give in. When a parent gives in to a child's temper tantrum, it teaches the child that 'If he throws a fit in the future, he will get his way.' Even worse would be to occasionally give in to a temper tantrum. Inconsistency is very confusing for children, yet they learn it very quickly. Set the boundaries and stick to them. Children will learn to adjust and to obey what is expected of them if we are consistent. It helps them learn to obey God later!

Create a bedtime routine. Take a bath, brush teeth (then parent checks and finishes the brushing). Say a Bible verse and read and/or watch Bible story (see Parent Cue app or Bible stories on Kids YouTube). Say prayers together as a family. Hug and kiss, turn out light, and shut the door.

Baby will probably still be in a crib that he cannot get out of. Lower the mattress to the floor if necessary, and he will develop the habit of falling asleep in his own room. At first, it may be necessary to start with rocking the baby to sleep while singing a soothing song and then putting him in his crib. This later leads to the habit of going to sleep alone.

Talk to the baby and tell him, "Tonight you are going to sleep in your crib (or bed). After your bedtime story and prayer, I am going to lay you in your crib to go to sleep on your own."

I was told to always remember that I would sleep better and so will the baby if we slept in our own beds. That helped me to keep pushing this concept until it happened as a matter of course.

GIFT IDEAS:

NOTE the <u>underlined</u> <u>and</u> <u>boldfaced</u> items in developmental lists. There are additional gift ideas in the **GIFT IDEAS** section at the end of the chapter.

- Crayons and paper
- Blocks
- Sturdy picture books or books with few words and lots of pictures to talk about
- Cooking and kitchen toys, fruits and vegetables with Velcro and a wooden knife for "cutting" fruits, veggies, and breads
- Musical toys
- Graduated rings or cups to stack

CHAPTER 28

I HAVE TO WATCH HIM EVERY MINUTE NOW!

12 to 18 Months

Around one year, a child can crawl up steps, push himself on a riding toy, and hold a cube. He can greet others when given verbal cues like, "Say Hi!"

He can also pull off his socks, chew most table foods well, and hold a cup.

GIFT IDEAS:

NOTE the <u>underlined</u> <u>and</u> <u>boldfaced</u> items in developmental lists below.

There are additional gift ideas in the **GIFT IDEAS** section at the end of the chapter.

<u>PHYSICAL - GROSS MOTOR</u>

13 Months

- Throws **<u>ball</u>** standing or sitting
- Stoops and recovers – bends down from standing position and regains standing without support
- Assumes and maintains kneeling – can support full body weight on knees

15 Months

- Walks alone, seldom falls
- Crawls up several steps – creeping (on hands and knees)

- Gets from sitting to standing position without using hands
- Demonstrates balance reaction when tilted while in kneeling position
- Stands from lying on back by getting on all fours and then rising to standing position without support
- Walks sideways
- Bends over and looks through legs
- Pushes self forward on **riding toy**

16 Months

- Stands on one foot with slight support
- Walks upstairs with one hand held
- Walks 3 feet on an 8-inch **board** or **plank** with someone holding one hand

18 Months

- Climbs into adult chair, turns to sit
- Backs self into **small chair**
- Runs
- Pushes and pulls large objects
- Throws **beanbag(s)** overhand
- Demonstrates balanced reactions when tilting while standing
- Carries large toy while walking
- Rolls like log

PHYSICAL - FINE MOTOR

14 Months

- Scribbles vigorously in imitation
- Unwraps toy
- Inserts **round block** into **round shape sorting toy**
- Holds 3 **cubes**

15 Months

- Puts many objects into container without removing any

16 Months

- Puts **large beads** in a box
- Obtains peg from bottle or **cup**
- Builds tower using 2 **cubes**
- Places 1 **round peg** in **pegboard**
- Points with index finger

17 Months

- Attains toy with stick
- Builds tower of 3 to 4 cubes

18 Months

- Places 10 cubes in cup
- Scribbles spontaneously
- Inverts small container to obtain tiny object after demonstration
- Uses one hand to hold toy and other hand manipulates, or explores toy
- Turns pages of **cardboard book**

COGNITIVE

13 Months

- Looks in appropriate place when asked, "Where is the ball?"

14 Months

- Unwraps toy
- Responds to simple verbal requests
- Demonstrates drinking from a **cup**
- Enjoys looking at pictures in books
- Imitates several new gestures
- Hands toy back to adult
- Holds 3 cubes

15 Months

- Asks for objects by pointing and vocalizing
- Overcomes simple objectives

16 Months

- Obtains peg from bottle
- Identifies self in mirror
- Identifies one body part

17 Months

- Attains toy with stick

18 Months

- Looks at picture book and turns pages

LANGUAGE

13 Months

- Looks in appropriate place when asked, "Where is the ball?"
- Imitates simple sounds on request
- Shows understanding of words by appropriate behavior or gesture
- Uses single-word sentences
- Pays attention to adult voices speaking
- Uses language intentionally and purposefully as a tool for communication

15 Months

- Uses jargon or jabbering but directed at others
- Greets with verbal cues
- Uses exclamatory expressions "o-o-o", "no-no"
- Says "no" meaningfully
- Babbles in response to human voice
- Uses expressive vocabulary, 1 to 3 words
- Uses nouns since he hears more nouns than other parts of speech

- Verbs are likely to appear next, followed by adjectives and adverbs
- Points and vocalizes to indicate wants

16 Months

- Attempts to sing sounds to **music**
- Uses 10-15 words spontaneously
- Vocalizes wishes and needs at the table: names desired items

17 Months

- Omits final and some initial consonants
- Uses subject and predicate phrase "dog run"
- Babbles statements, scolds, asks questions, tells stories, all without words, but with eloquent inflection, pitch and rhythm
- Sometimes indicates toilet needs
- Experiments with communication – not frustrated if not understood
- Points to pictures in book
- Names 1 object
- Follows 2 directions
- Points to 1 body part when asked

SELF CARE

13 Months

- Chews food with munching pattern

14 Months

- Chews most food well
- Pulls off socks

15 Months

- Climbs stairs on hands and knees
- Brings spoon to mouth – turns spoon over

- Holds cup handle
- Shows wet or soiled pants
- Overcomes simple objects
- Vocalizes and gestures to indicate wants

16 Months

- Holds cup and drinks with some spilling
- Imitates housework
- Removes hat

17 Months

- Fetches or carries familiar objects

18 Months

- Walks upstairs with one hand held
- Places edibles in mouth
- Moves about house without adults
- Hands empty dish to adult when finished eating
- Unzips zippers
- Gets onto adult chair unaided
- Uses toilet when taken by adult
- May refuse food as appetite decreases
- Holds and drinks from cup with some spilling
- Shows bowel control pattern
- Indicates discomfort over soiled pants verbally or by gesture
- Sleeps nights 10 to12 hours
- Naps once in afternoon 1 to 3 hours
- Removes socks
- Places hat on head
- Sucks from straw
- Chews semi-solid and solid food

SOCIAL - EMOTIONAL

13 Months

- Likes to be in constant sight and hearing of adult (12 to 13 months)

- Gives toy to familiar adult spontaneously and upon request (12 to 15 months)

15 Months

- Displays independent behavior; is difficult to discipline – the "no" stage
- Acts impulsively, unable to recognize rules
- Attempts self-direction; resists adult control
- Plays ball cooperatively
- Shows toy preferences
- Displays distractible behavior
- Hugs and kisses parents

18 Months

- May show fear and insecurity with previously accepted situations
- Displays frequent tantrum behaviors
- Needs and expects rituals and routines
- Begins to show a sense of humor – laughs at incongruities
- Enjoys imitating adult behavior: responds well to the introduction of new tasks
- Tends to be quite messy
- Enjoys being center of attention in family group
- Imitates doing housework, like vacuuming or dusting
- Smiles responsively
- Works with adult (1 minute)

SPIRITUAL

Each Spiritual Section starts with 1-2 Scriptures to say aloud every night.

"LORD, You are my God; I will… praise Your name… You have done wonderful things…" Taken from Isaiah 25:1 (NIV)

"The Spirit of the Sovereign LORD is on me … to proclaim good news to the poor … to bind up the brokenhearted, to proclaim

freedom for the captives ... to proclaim the year of the LORD's favor..." portions of Isaiah 61:1–2 (NIV)

Pearls of Inspiration, wisdom, and grace upon grace for all the parents and grandparents doing the best that you can for the children.

- Comforted by parent singing "Jesus Loves Me" over and over when rocking to sleep
- Listens to a short Bible story or Parent Cue Bible story video at bedtime
- Puts hands together to pray at mealtime and bedtime (may even be able to repeat parent words of simple prayer)
- Enjoys church nursery when attending church with parents/family
- Listens to Steve Green CDs 'Hide 'em In Your Heart' Vol. 1 and 2 Amazon.com or Steve Green 'Hide 'em in Your Heart' Vol 1 on YouTube

Train Up a Child in the Way That He Should Go, but Make Sure You Are Going That Way Yourself.

RESPONSIBILITY MEASURES

- **Key Concept:** Make sure the child minds when you tell her something reasonable to do like, "Pick up your toy, please." If she doesn't, go take her hand and guide her to pick the toy up and put it where it belongs. Don't let up. Follow through every time it is needed!
- Hands empty dish to adult when finished eating
- Takes off socks
- Unzips zippers
- Says 'Thank you' when receives what she asked for
- Holds adult hand when required (near street, busy place, etc.)
- Can pick from 2 choices (Do you want to wear this shirt or this one? Do you like this ball or this one?) Parent should only provide choices they agree with.

GIFT IDEAS

NOTE the additional gift ideas that are <u>underlined</u> <u>and</u> <u>boldfaced</u> items within developmental lists.
More **GIFT IDEAS** are listed at the end of each chapter.

- Large ball for rolling
- Soft small ball for throwing
- Plastic riding toy
- Child-size broom and dustpan
- Soft child-size chair
- Colored blocks
- Cardboard books
- Round pegs in peg board
- Sturdy picture books
- Sippy cup with handle
- Small spoon to fit child's hand
- Shape shorter box (where cube only goes into the square hole, etc.)
- Bean bags (made of sturdy material sewn into rectangle and stuffed with rice or dried beans)

Parenting Tips:

THOUGHT FOR THE DAY:
Speak Blessings Over Your Children (See 2 versions below)
Proclaim the LORD's favor over your family.
Example "Thank you LORD for bringing us good health!"

Words are powerful.

They have the ability to set the direction for our lives. When they're spoken over us by someone who has authority, such as a parent, a coach, or a mentor; they can determine our destiny.

One reason some people aren't reaching their potential is they've never had blessings spoken over them. They've never had anyone declare what they can become, who God says they are, and how they have seeds of greatness. (Men in prison reported to a

Kairos teacher that they had never had such words spoken over them.)

The prophet Isaiah went around declaring God's favor, freedom, and victory. He says that all those who would receive this declaration, those who would let these words take root, would see it come to pass.

Hundreds of years later, Jesus read this same declaration to the people in the synagogue in Nazareth. "The Spirit of the Lord is upon me to declare."

Jesus declares victory, abundance, healing, and freedom over you. If you receive it, He will put you on a path to greater joy, to better health, to stronger relationships, and to new levels of your destiny.

"IT HAS BEEN DECLARED!"
(Speak this blessing over your child often.)

"The LORD bless you and keep you;
The LORD make His face shine on you and be gracious;
The LORD turn His face toward you and give you peace."
Numbers 6:24-26 NIV

"The LORD bless you and keep you;
May the LORD smile on you and be gracious to you;
May the LORD show you His favor and give you His peace."
Numbers 6:24-26 NLT

If you need help for yourself and your children to be able to take a stand for your family's Christian values in education and in the world, contact us for a free 1-on-1 Strategy Session: edempower777@gmail.com

CHAPTER 29

SHE'S TALKING SO-O-O MUCH! WHAT SHOULD I BE TEACHING HER?

18 TO 24 MONTHS

During this stage, most children respond to words, identify objects that are similar or different, imitate actions and language of adults, point out familiar objects and people in pictures in a book.

For physical development, they can walk backwards, color or paint by moving the entire arm, scribble, turn knobs and handles, walk up and down stairs without help, and move and sway to music. They are becoming more creative and are developing a sense of humor.

GIFT IDEAS:

NOTE the additional gift ideas that are <u>underlined</u> <u>and</u> <u>boldfaced</u> items within developmental lists.
More **GIFT IDEAS** are listed at the end of each chapter.

<u>PHYSICAL - GROSS MOTOR</u>

19 Months

- Carries large **<u>teddy</u> <u>bear</u>** or **<u>doll</u>** while walking
- Walks independently on **<u>8-inch</u> <u>wide</u> <u>board</u>** or **<u>plank</u>**

21 Months

- Creeps backward downstairs
- Walks with one foot on walking board

- Walks downstairs with hand held
- Squats and play
- Walks backward

24 Months

- Jumps in place – both feet
- Walks approximately on line
- Jumps from bottom step
- Kicks ball without losing balance
- Picks an object from floor without falling
- Stands on tiptoes
- Stands from lying on back by rolling to side, sits up, then stands without assistance
- Walks upstairs holding rail, both feet on step
- Runs fairly well

PHYSICAL - FINE MOTOR

19 Months

- Inverts small container spontaneously to obtain tiny object
- Places 6 **round pegs in pegboard**

21 Months

- Builds tower of 5-6 **cubes**

22 Months

- Puts 3 shapes in correct hole (circle, square, and triangle) of **shape sorter toy**
- Completes 3-piece **puzzle**
- **Stacks rings on spindle**

23 Months

- Strings one 1-inch **bead(s)**
- Stirs

24 Months

- Attempts to fold **paper**

- Builds tower of 6 to 7 cubes
- Imitates vertical stroke
- Imitates circular stroke
- Turns pages of book
- Turns shape to put in correct hole with 4 trials
- Unscrews 3-inch lid

COGNITIVE

21 Months

- Builds tower of 5 to 6 cubes
- Follows simple single directions
- Names two objects

22 Months

- Child completes 3-piece formboard (circle, square, and triangle)
- Attempts and then succeeds in activating **mechanical toy**
- Uses **playdough** and **paints**
- **Paste**s on one side
- Paints within limits of **paper**
- Matches sounds to animals

24 Months

- Names 3 objects
- Builds tower of 6 to7 cubes
- Refers to self by name
- Comprehends and asks for "another" or "more"
- Names 3 pictures
- Points to 4 body parts
- Leads adult to what he wants in next room
- Hands objects similar to familiar sample
- Explores cabinets and drawers
- Matches objects to picture
- Sorts objects
- Assembles 4 **nesting blocks**

- Recognizes self in photograph
- Remembers where objects belong
- Turns pages one at a time
- Matches sounds to pictures of animals
- Identifies 6 body parts
- Turns shape around to fit correctly in hole in four trials
- Uses simple 2-word sentences
- Shows three body parts upon request
- Attempts activation of **mechanical toy** after demonstration
- Sorts two different types of objects by shape (same color)
- Points to 5 pictures
- Scribble is circular
- Vertical and horizontal line imitated 2 out of 3 times
- Forces tops on boxes without regard for shape of box
- Retrieves toy from regular places

LANGUAGE

19 Months

- Names one picture
- Points to 3 pictures when asked
- Vocalizes or gestures spontaneously to indicate needs
- Uses voice in conjunction with pointing or gesturing
- Jabbers tunefully at play
- Echoes prominent or last words spoken

21 Months

- Speaks 20 words
- Names two objects or pictures
- Follows 3 directions
- Asks for food when hungry, may ask for toilet or drink also
- Speaks in 2-word sentences

- Makes sound in babbling, but often substitutes those sounds in words
- Imitates environmental sounds (such as animals or vehicles)

22 Months

- Uses jargon with good inflection and rate

23 Months

- Attempts to sing songs with words

24 Months

- Names 3 objects
- Refers to self by name
- Comprehends and asks for "another" or "more"
- Names 3 pictures
- Points to 5 pictures when asked to do so
- Points to 4 body parts
- Understands 2 of these prepositions "on," "in," "under," "behind," "in front of" when used in sentences combining with nouns and verbs in 2-word sentences
- Expresses needs with increased frequency
- Continues the spontaneous modification of pronunciation of words to fit his own vocalization pattern
- Expressive language behind receptive, but may have speaking vocabulary of 50 words
- Repetitions in words and phrases are frequent

SELF CARE

21 Months

- Creeps backward
- Steps upstairs with hand on rail
- Replaces some objects where they belong

22 Months

- Puts shoes on partway
- Unwraps food

24 Months

- Takes off clothes with help
- Pulls pants or shorts on and off
- Dries own hands
- Scoops food, feeds self with spoon with some spilling
- Distinguishes between edible and inedible objects
- Chews completely with rotary jaw movements
- Gives up bottle
- Removes shoes when laces undone
- Requests food by word or gesture
- Sits on potty chair or on adaptive seat on toilet with assistance
- May be toilet regulated by adult – bladder controlled
- Plays with food
- Washes and dries hands partially
- Anticipates need to eliminate – uses same word for both functions
- Opens doors by turning knob
- Helps with simple household tasks
- May have definite food preferences
- Drinks from glass held in one hand

SOCIAL - EMOTIONAL

22 Months

- Learns culturally acceptable behaviors (including toilet training and cleanliness)
- Carries doll around
- Enjoys **pull**ing **toys**
- Puts own possessions where belong
- Resistant to changes and sudden transition
- Imitates actions of adults; reading paper, sweeping, dusting, washing car

24 Months

- Expresses affection
- Shows jealousy at attention given to others, especially other family members
- Shows a wide variety of emotions: fear, anger, sympathy, modesty, guilt, embarrassment, anxiety, joy
- Desires control of others – orders, fights, resists
- Interacts with peers using gestures
- Engages in parallel play – beside or around other children, but with little interaction
- Enjoys solitary play coloring, building, looking at picture books for a few minutes
- Enjoys rough-and-tumble play
- Experiences a strong sense of self-importance
- Attempts to comfort others in distress
- Defends possessions
- Takes direction from non-family member
- Works with adult (5 minutes)
- Needs lots of praise for development of positive self-concept

SPIRITUAL

Each Spiritual Section starts with 2 Scriptures to say aloud every night.

"I will sing to the LORD as long as I live." Psalm 104: 33 (NLT)

"The fear of the LORD is the beginning of wisdom." Psalm 111:10 (NASB)

- Child puts hands together (may need reminder) as we pray at meals and bedtime
- Child repeats a short prayer that parent says as the child begins to talk
- Memorizes short verses to say with pictures and motions:

*"Praise Him, **sun** and **moon**, praise Him, all you **shining stars!**"* Psalm 148:3 N(IV) (Raise arms for 'praise.' Print out pictures for 'sun,' 'moon,' and 'stars' and put into the verse printed on a paper as a reminder until the verse is memorized.)

Important Note:

According to Baptist Press:

- If a child leads the way in going to church, only **3.5 %** of families will follow.
- If the mother leads her family to church, **17%** of the families will follow.
- **BUT IF DAD LEADS THE WAY, 93% of the families will follow.**

RESPONSIBILITY MEASURES

- Child says "Thank You" as appropriate
- Helps with simple household tasks
- Picks up a toy and puts it where it belongs. At first, the parent may need to take the child's hand and guide them to pick up the toy while talking about where it goes and walking the child there to release the toy in the correct cubby or shelf.

Parenting Tips:

Take a picture of medical toys. Print out the picture and tape it to the correct cubby with packaging tape as a visual cue of where all the medical toys go. Do this for each drawer and cubby, so that everything has a place. This will help children learn to clean up and keep things organized.

Dr. James Dobson stated that what children need from parents during the developmental years is an understanding of who God is and what He expects them to do. This teaching must begin very early in childhood.

God made wonderful things, just as He created each one of us. Even at two years old a child is capable of learning that the flowers, the sky, the birds, and even the rainbows are gifts from God's hand.

GIFT IDEAS:

NOTE the additional gift ideas that are <u>underlined</u> <u>and</u> <u>boldfaced</u> items within developmental lists.
More **GIFT IDEAS** are listed at the end of each chapter.

- Teddy bear
- Soft doll
- 2X4 board to practice walking and balancing on
- Medium ball for kicking
- Round pegs and pegboard (to match colors, to, count, or to add)
- Colored cubes
- Shape sorter box with cube/cylinder/triangle to put in correct hole
- 3 to 4 piece wooden puzzle with large knobs
- Crayons and paper
- Thick shoe string with 1-inch wooden beads
- Play-doh
- Paint
- Paste
- Paper
- Foam board with shapes cut out
- Mechanical toy
- Pull toy that makes animal sounds with picture
- Nesting blocks
- Graduated rings on a peg
- Song books
- Pull toy
- Sturdy picture or books with 1 to 2 sentences on a page
- Toy with animal picture and sounds to match

If you need help for yourself and your children to be able to take a stand for your family's Christian values in education and in the world, contact us for a free 1-on-1 Strategy Session: <u>edempower777@gmail.com</u>

Education Empowerment Coach
Susan Perez

CHAPTER 30

NO! MINE! THANK YOU! PLEASE!

2 TO 3 YEARS

Most 2-year-old toddlers become very independent. They are better able to explore the world. Most of the learning as a toddler results from their own experiences.

For cognitive skills, they can sort objects by category, stack toys from largest to smallest, respond to simple directions, name familiar objects, match objects, engage in fantasy play, identify self in a mirror, say names including own name.

For physical development, they start to run, jump in place, kick a ball, stand on one foot, turn the page in a book, draw a circle, and hold a crayon between the thumb and finger.

GIFT IDEAS:

NOTE the additional gift ideas that are <u>underlined</u> and <u>boldfaced</u> items within developmental lists.
More **GIFT IDEAS** are listed at the end of each chapter.

<u>PHYSICAL - GROSS MOTOR</u>

26 Months

- Throws <u>**bean bag**</u> at least 5 feet overhanded from a sitting position
- Goes up and down slide
- Catches <u>**large ball**</u>
- Walks downstairs holding rail, both feet on step
- Stands on <u>**2-inch balance beam**</u> with both feet for 2 to 3 seconds

28 Months

- Walks downstairs alone – both feet on step
- Jumps backward
- Walks backward 10 feet
- Stands momentarily on each foot

30 Months

- Alternates feet while walking upstairs with support
- Rides **tricycle** – sometimes propelling with feet on ground
- Jumps a distance of 8 to 14 inches
- Runs – stops without holding and avoids obstacles
- Imitates one foot standing
- Walks on tiptoes a few seconds
- Jumps on **trampoline** with adult holding hands

32 Months

- Jumps sideways
- Alternates steps on 2-inch balance beam
- Stands from lying using a sit up

36 Months

- Hops on one foot – 2 or more hops
- Walks up and down stairs alternating feet
- Balances on one foot
- Jumps 14 to 24 inches
- Walks on tiptoes 10 feet
- Walks on line for 10 feet
- Uses pedals on tricycle alternately
- Climbs **jungle gyms** and ladders
- Catches **8-inch ball**
- Runs on toes
- Makes sharp turns around corners when running

PHYSICAL - FINE MOTOR

25 Months

- Holds **crayon** with thumb and fingers
- Strings 3 **one-inch beads**
- Holds **scissors**

27 Month

- Makes train of **cubes**
- Imitates drawing vertical line, horizontal line, and circle

30 Months

- Builds tower of 8 cubes
- Holds **pencil** with thumb and forefinger instead of fist
- Imitates drawing a cross or plus sign
- Puts tiny object into small container
- Folds paper in half
- Places 6 **square pegs in pegboard**
- Turns doorknob

33 Months

- Build tower of 10 cubes
- Imitates "bridge" of blocks
- **Strings half-inch beads**

35 Months

- Makes first designs of spontaneous forms
- Snips on a line with scissors (with assistance)
- Builds tower using 9 cubes

36 Months

- Copies circle
- Adapts to form board reversal – turns shape to fit in correct hole
- Adds 2 parts to incomplete person
- Cuts across paper with scissors (crooked) with assistance
- Unscrews one-inch lid

<u>**COGNITIVE**</u>

27 Months

- Makes train of cubes
- Imitates drawing vertical line, horizontal line, and circle
- Repeats 2 digits
- Understands size differences
- Identifies clothing items for different occasions
- Enjoys **tactile books**
- Identifies rooms in own house
- Demonstrates use of objects
- Finds details in favorite **picture book**
- Recognizes familiar adult in **photograph book**
- Engages in simple make-believe activities
- Knows more body parts
- Selects pictures involving action words
- Obeys two part commands
- Understands complex and compound sentences

30 Months

- Shows or tells use of one or more familiar objects on request
- Names or identifies objects by use
- Builds tower of 8 cubes
- Points to 7 pictures when named "Where's the ___?"
- Names 5 pictures on a card when asked "What is this?"
- Can draw cross in imitation
- Gives full name
- Readily turns shape around to fit in hole
- Enjoys **nursery rhymes, nonsense rhymes, finger plays, poetry**
- Unscrews lids from jars
- Strings 3 large beads with long, tipped lace
- Understands 2 - Gives two blocks in response to 2 fingers
- Understands many action verbs
- Identifies objects when described in terms of function: drink from, wear on foot, and eat cereal with

- Identifies body parts with their function
- Matches objects to objects
- Matches picture to pictures
- Inconsistently matches a few colors

33 Months

- Names or points to self in photograph
- Responds correctly to "show me one block" (or finger)
- Builds tower of 10 cubes
- Imitates "bridge" of blocks

36 Months

- Holds regular crayon with fingertips
- Snips with **children's scissors** (crooked) with assistance
- Strings **small beads**
- Turns the handle on a **Jack-in-the-box** 3 revolutions without letting go
- **Hammers** a **peg toy**
- Clips close pins on a can
- Looks at books independently
- Stacks rings in correct order
- Plays with **water** and **sand**
- Completes **3** to **4-piece puzzle**
- Lines blocks up by color groups
- Matches 4 colors of blocks to matching colored bowls
- Matches several common objects to bright simplified pictures of each
- Plays house
- Can distinguish "longer" and "shorter"

LANGUAGE

27 Months

- Sings phrases of songs
- Produces the following consonant sounds clearly: p, b, m, k, g, w, h, n, t, d.
- Imitates spontaneously or requests new words

28 Months

- Experiments with communication – frustrated when not understood

30 Months

- Uses 3-word sentences
- Uses past tense
- Repeats 2 digits
- Uses size words
- Adds "ing" endings to words
- Uses plurals
- Tells or shows use of one or more familiar objects on request
- Names or identifies objects by use
- Names 5 pictures
- Points to 7 pictures named
- Gives full name when asked

SELF CARE

30 Months

- Dries own hands
- Helps carry and put things away
- Turns faucet on and off
- Delays sleeping by demanding things
- Holds **small cup** in one hand
- Puts on shoes with assistance
- Understands and stays away from common dangers – stairs, glass, strange animals
- Holds spoon in fingers – palms up
- Washes hands
- Wipes nose with assistance
- May reject many foods
- May awaken crying from dreams

33 Months

- Dresses with supervision
- Puts on coat unassisted
- Helps with bathing self

34 Months

- Puts on shirt or dress unassisted
- Blows nose with assistance

36 Months

- Walks up and down stairs using alternating feet
- Pours well from pitcher
- Puts on shoes
- Undresses completely without help
- Unbuttons front buttons
- Insists on doing things independently
- Knows proper place for things
- Uses fork
- Uses napkins
- Hangs clothing on hook
- Buttons large buttons
- Dries hands
- Distinguishes between urination and bowel movements
- Serves self at table with little spilling
- Shows interest in setting table
- Verbalizes need to use toilet – has occasional accidents
- Takes responsibility for toileting; requires assistance in wiping
- Sleeps 10 to15 hours daily

SOCIAL - EMOTIONAL

30 Months

- Works in small group (5 minutes)
- Plays cooperative (shares) with other children

- Fatigues easily
- Dawdles and procrastinates
- Values own property; uses word "mine"
- Takes pride in clothing
- Becoming aware of sex differences
- May develop sudden fears, especially of large animals
- Holds parent's hand outdoors
- Displays dependent behavior; clings and whines
- Dramatizes using a doll
- Says "no," but submits anyway
- Tends to be physically aggressive
- Enjoys experimenting with adult activities

- Frustration tantrums peak
- Demands to take toys to bed
- Enjoys drinking from fountain
- Able to wait a few minutes to delay gratification
- Does not share but finds substitute toys
- Adjusts play behavior to partner's ability
- Mimics actions of others
- Warmly responsive to adults
- Imagination entering into play

RESPONSIBILITY MEASURES

At this age, it might seem easier to just pick up your child's toys for them, but some day parents will tire of doing that. Each child needs to learn to be a part of the family and have the satisfaction of doing a few chores to help out.

If we just GIVE things to our child, they do not feel the satisfaction of a job well done. Also, learning to do a job well helps to build confidence, develop interests, and identify talents.

- When asked to choose between 2 items, child can point to or express which one he wants (Do you want to wear this shirt or that one? Child can point to or indicate one and be happy, even pleased, to put it on.)
- Places paper towel into waste basket
- Dries own hands
- Helps carry and put things away
- Puts on shoes with assistance
- Washes and dries hands
- Wipes nose with assistance
- Dresses with supervision
- Puts on shirt or dress unassisted
- Helps bathe self
- Puts on coat, no assistance (33 months)
- Undresses completely without help
- Puts on shoes/ takes off shoes and socks
- Hangs clothing on hook
- Holds parent's hand outdoors, as needed
- Mimics actions of others
- Warmly responds to adults
- Imagination enters into play

SPIRITUAL

Each Spiritual Section starts with 2 Scriptures to say aloud every night. Parents can add to these as the year goes on.

"Fear of (respect for) the LORD is the beginning of wisdom." Psalm 111:10 (NASB)

"You are my God, and I give thanks to You." Psalm 118:28 (NASB)

- Listens to bedtime story read from Beginners Bible and/or video of Bible story on the Parent Cue app or Bible story on YouTube Kids
- Repeats a short Bible verse each night
- Puts hands together and repeats short phrases of parent's prayer at dinner or bedtime

- Listens and give a short response to family devotional time
- Attends church (nursery) with family
- Does **Dirty Water Experiment** with parent (below)

Dirty Water Experiment*

- o Fill a clear glass half full of water. Put a few drops of red, yellow and green (to make brown) food coloring into the glass to represent our sin.
- o Put a few drops of bleach into the water.
- o Explain how this is like what God will do in our hearts when we believe in Jesus and ask Him to forgive our sins. *by Josh Mulvihill

As parents and teachers, we are here to equip, encourage, and inspire our children and to raise them to know, fear, and love the LORD. May they come to know Him early in life and use their lives for Christ!

Parenting Tips:

Around AGE 2, children learn how to say "no" - a lot! So avoid saying, "Let's clean up now," to which the child responds, "No."

Instead, try starting a question with, "Is there any reason why?" which needs a "no " answer. For example, "Is there any reason we shouldn't clean up now?" "No" "Great, let's put up the dress-up clothes."

Start giving your 2-year-old choices. That means 2 choices that you could live with either. This gives your child a measure of independence and responsibility. For example, "Do you want to wear this shirt or that one? Do you want to take a bath or brush your teeth first?"

A firm, constant bedtime routine is important to help a child be ready to fall asleep peacefully. This plan could include potty, wash hands, brush teeth, bathe, put own dirty clothes into the laundry, put own carefully closed up diaper in the trash, listen to a bedtime story (ask what color the ball is or what sound a cow makes to keep the child engaged), and pray together.

Then, some children may need you to lay down with them a few minutes while reading the bedtime story and praying. Others may be fine if parents just make sure they have their favorite stuffed animal and give them a hug and a kiss, before saying goodnight.

GIFT IDEAS:

NOTE the additional gift ideas that are <u>underlined</u> <u>and</u> <u>boldfaced</u> items within developmental lists.
More **GIFT IDEAS** are listed at the end of each chapter.

- Bean bags
- Children's Bible
- Tricycle
- Jungle gym with ladders
- Large crayons
- Fiskar blunt scissors or other scissors with 'spring' to re-open after each cut
- Child-sized trampoline with side netting
- Large ball, 1-foot by 2-foot board or plank that measures 6 feet long to use as a balance beam

CHAPTER 31

NOW IT'S TIME TO EXPOSE MY CHILD TO AS MUCH QUALITY EDUCATION AS POSSIBLE!

3 TO 4 YEARS

Children 3 to 4 years old can understand more complex ideas. They sort through what they see in the world around them. Children wonder how things work and why.

They often understand past and future events. They can ride a tricycle or a scooter, go down a slide without help, throw and catch a ball, pull and steer toys, build tall towers with blocks, and manipulate **<u>clay</u>** into shapes.

GIFT IDEAS:

NOTE the additional gift ideas that are <u>underlined</u> <u>and</u> <u>boldfaced</u> items within developmental lists.
More **GIFT IDEAS** are listed at the end of each chapter.

<u>PHYSICAL – GROSS MOTOR</u>

36 Months

- Jumps with both feet from standing position
- Stands with heels together and arms at side
- Plays running games
- Stands on one foot – one second
- Walks on line
- Catches **<u>ball</u>** with extended stiff arms

- Carries tray
- Pedals **tricycle**
- Jumps vertically with both feet
- Walks upstairs alternate feet with aid
- Catches **9-inch ball** arms and body
- Throws 9-inch ball, underhand

40 Months

- Walks downstairs, alternate feet with aid
- Skips
- Bounces 9-inch ball 4 to 5 feet
- Jumps 10 or more steps

42 Months

- Walks upstairs alternate feet
- Throws **tennis ball** 5 feet
- Uses **fingerpaints** with whole hand

44 Months

- Draws man with head, legs, and trunk

48 Months

- Carries a cup of water
- Walks on circular line
- Stands on one foot, 5 seconds
- Hops on one foot about 7 steps
- Walks forward heel-to-toe
- Skips on one foot (gallops)
- Throws ball overhand, 10 feet
- Catches ball with arms bent at elbows
- Pedals tricycle around obstacles and sharp corners
- Climbs ladders and playground equipment
- Runs to line and jumps over with both feet
- Somersaults
- Walks downstairs alternate feet
- Cuts with **scissors,** not necessarily constructively

- Plays running games
- Can extend arms and twist trunk
- Runs smoothly with speed
- Jumps vertically - 12 inches
- Ascends stairs using alternating feet

PHYSICAL - FINE MOTOR

36 Months

- Builds 3 block bridge after demonstration
- Builds tower of 10 **cubes**
- Closes fist and wiggles thumb, right and left
- Stirs liquid with spoon
- Picks up small object with tongs
- Folds and creases paper horizontally and vertically
- Turns handle on **pencil sharpener**
- Unscrews 1-inch lid
- Cuts 6-inch paper in two

40 Months

- Winds up toy
- Stacks six graduated blocks by size
- Cuts 6-inch line within one half inch, 15 seconds

42 Months

- Makes flat round cake from **clay**
- Rolls "snake" from clay
- Makes ball out of clay
- Winds up toy
- Copies circle, and letters H, V, and T
- Traces diamond shape

46 Months

- Completes house by adding one detail
- Draws a man with two parts

48 Months

- Cuts with scissors along drawn straight line
- Prints 3 capital letters from model
- Spreads fingers on one hand and touch fingers (one at a time) to thumb of same hand
- Folds paper and creases vertically, horizontally, and diagonally
- Completes **3-piece puzzle**
- Feeds self with spoon without undue spills (liquid, semi-solids, solids)
- Gets drink of water without help
- Unfastens, unzips, unbuttons and removes all but very difficult clothing
- Puts on all clothes except for fastenings
- May have trouble with heel of socks
- Shoes may be on wrong feet
- Unable to lace or tie shoes
- Holds paper in place while other hand writes
- Finger paints using arm, hands, and fingers
- Holds brush with thumb and fingers instead of fist
- Screws on one-inch lid
- Grasps **pencil** with finger
- Cuts 2-inch triangle within 1/2 inch, 45 seconds
- Sorts objects (nuts from bolts)
- Traces along line

COGNITIVE

36 Months

- Sorts **cubes** of two colors
- Repeats 3 digits
- Counts by rote to 3
- Gives 2 objects
- Points to "big" object
- Gives "both" objects

- Points to "different" objects
- Demonstrates use of familiar objects
- Points to fingers, toes, stomach, back, knee, chin

42 Months

- Points to "empty" object
- Matches 2 colors
- Counts 3 objects
- Points to "small" square
- Places ring on stacked toy according to size
- Points to "long" objects
- Names familiar melody
- Classifies pictures by pointing
- Matches sets of objects

48 Months

- Matches 4 colors
- Gives "heavy" object
- Points to "rough" and "smooth" textures
- Discriminates verbal absurdities by answering questions
- Points to picture of "tall" object
- Matches related pictures
- Counts by rote to 10
- Names missing object
- Follows sequentially a series of pictures
- Points to teeth, heels, fingernails
- Names primary colors (red, yellow, blue)
- Compares weight (heavy, light)
- Matches quantity of blocks or small objects: 3, 4, 5
- Sorts 3 sizes of objects
- Selects cubes matching a pattern
- Assembles **10 nesting cups** through trial and error
- Puts together 2 halves of simple picture
- Imitates a square: corners rounded
- Recognizes time (day or night) in pictures
- Recognizes all major colors

36 Months

- Names preferred object
- Points to 10 **pictures** of **common objects**
- Names 8 pictures of common objects
- Names 3 pictures of common actions
- Says (or sings) words to **nursery rhymes** or **songs**
- Answers one question regarding physical needs
- Uses personal pronouns – I, you, and me
- Speaks "intelligently"
- Talks on telephone
- Refers to others by pronoun
- Selects correct pronoun (him, he, his)
- Uses negative phrases
- Tells own sex
- Tells full name
- Tells age

43 Months

- Names 10 pictures of common objects
- Demonstrates understanding of 3 prepositions by placing cube
- Responds to "how" and "where" questions
- Delivers one-part verbal message
- Answers "if - what" questions
- Shows interest in conversation of others

48 Months

- Consonants/k/, /s/, /sh/, /v/, /j/, /r/, and some double and triple consonants, /pl/, /mp/, /mpt/, are usually mastered by this age
- Discriminates "is" and "is not" by pointing to objects
- Demonstrates understanding of 4 prepositions by placing cube

- Tells uses of objects
- Uses prepositions
- Answers questions regarding physical needs
- Repeats 12-syllable sentence
- Requests one item from store clerk
- Gives account of recent experience in order of accuracy
- Tells street address
- Names siblings
- Forms questions spontaneously
- Describes action in pictures
- Uses "the" in speech
- Uses past tense (I jumped)
- Uses connecting verbs (forms of 'be') - I "am" home; I "am" a boy
- Uses complex sentence structure more frequently
- Answers simple questions with 3 or more words
- Comprehends demonstrative pronouns: this, that, these
- Comprehends adjectives
- Comprehends negative (not jumping)

SELF CARE

36 Months

- Feeds self with fork (held with fist)
- Holds cup by handle when drinking
- Wipes nose with tissue
- Turns faucet on and off
- Turns doorknob and opens door
- Pours from pitcher
- Removes pull-down garment
- Unties and removes shoes
- Unbottons buttons
- Undresses completely, with assistance
- Removes pull-over garment
- Puts on **shoes** (often wrong feet)

- Snaps front snaps
- Brushes teeth with assistance
- Uses spoon in fist, no spilling

42 Months

- Walks to classroom from bus/play area
- Gets drink of water
- Washes and dries hands
- Unbuckles belt
- Flushes toilet after toileting
- Goes to toilet alone
- Dresses with supervision
- Cleans up spills with help
- Eliminates with few accidents

48 Months

- Places paper towel into waste basket
- Puts on sock
- Zips non-separating front zipper
- Serves food to self
- Prepares bowl of dry cereal
- Puts on pull-up garment
- Buckles belt
- Buttons front buttons
- Puts on shoes (on correct feet)
- Laces shoes
- Dresses completely without assistance
- Brushes teeth without assistance
- Feeds self with spoon (held with fingers)
- Wipes self with assistance after toileting
- Sucks from plastic straw
- Uses napkin
- Wipes mouth with napkin when reminded
- Distinguishes between front and back of clothes
- Hangs up coat on hook

- Washes and dries hands independently
- Bathes self with supervision: assistance required to clean thoroughly
- Applies toothpaste to brush
- Brushes hair independently
- Spreads soft foods on bread with knife
- Serves self from container

<u>SOCIAL - EMOTIONAL</u>

36 Months

- Responds to initial greeting
- Sits in circle and joins group in imitating leader
- Plays simple group games
- Puts toys away with supervision
- Shares toys
- Takes turns
- Listens "attentively" to stories
- Expresses displeasure verbally rather than physically
- Tells sex

42 Months

- Separates from parent easily
- Points to self in group photograph
- Performs for others
- Plays with other children (associative play)
- Asks permission to use items belonging to other people
- Works in small group – 15 minutes

48 Months

- Puts toys away without supervision
- Plays cooperatively with other children
- Participates in dramatic, make-believe play
- Says "Thank-you" for service or compliment

- Says "please" with request
- Goes on errands outside classroom
- Tells age
- Tells names of siblings
- Tells street name and address
- Waits to be acknowledged before speaking
- Plays table games with supervision
- Close relationships extended beyond family
- Tension outbursts exaggerated
- Demanding of adults
- Jealous of attention paid to others
- Engages in dramatic play

SPIRITUAL

Each Spiritual Section starts with several Scriptures to say aloud every night and memorize.

"Let your light shine before others, that they may see your good deeds and glorify your Father in heaven." Matthew 5:16b NIV (Teachable moment: Let my light shine, not to bring attention to me, but to bring attention to God!)

"Give thanks to the LORD, for He is good; His love endures forever." Psalm 118:29 (NIV)

"We have the LORD our God to help us." 2 Chronicles 32:8 (NLT)

"Let everything that has breath praise the LORD!" Psalm 150: 6a (NIV)

At this age, children have a growing sense that God is very real and special. They have a literal concept of God, perhaps as a "grandfather" figure. They sense that God loves and cares for them.

- Memorizes a short Bible verse (See Parent Cue app) by the end of each month
- Puts hands together and repeats short phrases of parent's prayer at dinner or bedtime
- Listens and gives a short response to family devotional time

- Watches Listener Kids on YouTube Kids with an adult
- Engages in dramatic play acting out Bible stories
- Creates a **Book of Colors** (below). Show your (grand)child the wordless book. Tell him it is a very important story, but there are no words in this book.

Book of Colors*

Parents: Using your own words, tell how the colors relate to the Gospel.

- **GOLD** = Heaven. Heaven is a beautiful place where no one gets sick. No one is sad. Heaven is God's home. God loves us very much and wants us to be with Him. There is something that would keep us from being with God. Rev. 21:4
- **BLACK**= Sin. Sin is not minding or obeying God and His laws. It is doing what we want instead of what God wants. Every person has sinned except Jesus. God is perfect and just. He does not ignore or excuse sin. Romans 3:23 and 6:23
- **RED** = The blood of Jesus. Jesus came and lived on the earth as a baby. He lived a perfect life. Jesus paid the penalty of sin by dying on the cross for our sins. Three days later He was raised from the dead. Romans 5:8 and John 3:16
- **WHITE** = Made clean. If we ask Jesus to forgive our sins, He will wash us white as snow. 1 John 1:9
- **GREEN** = Growing in Christ. It is important for us to grow in Christ by praying, reading the Bible, obeying God, and going to church. We should also be kind to people and help them out.

Note:

Limit screen time to 30 minutes a day and an adult should supervise (sit with child) all screen time to make sure it's educational and wholesome. Screen time shortens the attention span. Children left unattended with a phone or iPad touch a new video about every minute or two and get in the habit of not finishing the videos.

<u>**RESPONSIBILITY MEASURES**</u>

(Some items are summarized from **SELF CARE** Section above.)

- Feeds self with fork or spoon
- Prepares bowl of dry cereal
- Wipes mouth with napkin when reminded
- Wipes nose with tissue
- Dresses and undresses completely with assistance (48 months)
- Snaps front snaps
- Hangs up coat on hook
- Puts on shoes (often wrong feet)
- Goes to toilet alone
- Flushes toilet after toileting
- Washes and dries hands independently
- Bathes self with supervision: assistance required to clean thoroughly
- Applies toothpaste and brushes teeth (parent checks)
- Brushes hair independently (may need help in the back)
- Spreads soft foods on bread with knife
- Serves self from container
- Tells street address
- Names siblings
- Puts toys away with supervision
- Shares toys
- Takes turns
- Listens "attentively" to stories
- Says "Thank-you" for service or compliment
- Says "please" with request
- Can bring parent something requested from another room
- Waits to be acknowledged before speaking, when appropriate

"If you follow through when they are 3, they'll believe you when they are 13!"

by <u>forthechildren.com</u>

Parenting Tips:

Three- and four-year-olds are ready to play Hide and Seek. This game begins as Peek-a-Boo and progresses to the 3-year-old hiding, but in plain sight.

Then by age 4, the child is ready to hide (maybe with an adult or older sibling until they learn some good hiding places and how to wait until we find them). The person who is 'It' finds them and can growl or say 'booo' which may cause lots of giggling.

Waiting to be found helps the child to learn **delayed gratification,** which is an important milestone that can be built upon throughout life!

Have your hungry child help prepare the meal or set the table instead of just providing a snack. The snack may ruin or dampen the child's appetite. Another option is to give a healthy snack like carrot sticks that the child can eat while helping prepare for the meal.

Waiting for the meal teaches **delayed gratification**, which helps with **steadfast determination**, **setting a goal** and working to reach it, and **taking self-initiative** as he goes through life!

Worship as a Family
Pray as a Family
Attend Church as a Family
Read the Bible as a Family
Pursue the LORD as a Family
Teach Them by Your Example!

GIFT IDEAS:

NOTE the additional gift ideas that are <u>underlined</u> <u>and</u> <u>boldfaced</u> items within developmental lists.

More **GIFT IDEAS** are listed at the end of each chapter.

- Tricycle or scooter
- Medium beach ball for playing catch
- Pull and steer toys
- Blocks for building tall towers
- Clay
- Fingerpaints and large fingerpaint paper
- Child-sized blunt scissors (Fischer)
- 3-5 piece puzzles
- Wind-up toy
- Picture puzzle cut into 3-4 pieces
- Action picture books to discuss
- Nursery rhyme books or songs
- Dress-up clothes for dramatic play
- Simple origami paper folding to be done with adult help
- Manual pencil sharpener to practice turning handle to sharpen pencils
- Objects to sort or match (such as nuts and bolts, different size or colored blocks, graduated rings on stacking toy)
- "Rough" and "smooth" textures to sort or match
- Musical toy to encourage singing along or naming familiar tunes

Books as Gifts:

William Lane Craig's Books "What is God Like?"

https://apologetics-store.biola.edu/products/what-is-god-like?variant= 32208630 415444

God is All-Good
God is All-Knowing
God is All-Loving
God is All-Powerful
God is Everywhere
God is Forever
God is Self-Sufficient
God is Spirit
God is Three Persons
The Greatness of God

If you need help for yourself and your children to be able to take a stand for your family's Christian values in education and in the world, contact us for a free 1-on-1 Strategy Session: edempower777@gmail.com

CHAPTER 32

I JUST CAN'T BELIEVE HOW SMART MY CHILD IS!

4 TO 5 YEARS

Children 4 to 5 years old develop independence, creativity, self-control, and self-confidence. Children this age become better at using words, imitating adult actions, counting objects, rhyming words, stating opposites, identifying many colors, and drawing pictures of people.

They can hop, walk backwards, turn somersaults, cut paper, print letters, and copy shapes. Their ability to express feelings and emotions develops.

GIFT IDEAS:

NOTE the gift ideas that are <u>underlined</u> <u>and</u> <u>boldfaced</u> items within the developmental lists.
More **GIFT IDEAS** are listed at the end of each chapter.

<u>PHYSICAL - GROSS MOTOR</u>

54 Months

- Hangs from bar
- Catches bounced **<u>ball</u>**

60 Months

- Can walk on tiptoe a long distance
- Jumps vertically 28 to 30 inches
- Hops 10 or more steps on one foot

- Climbs easily
- Skips on alternating feet
- Catches ball with both hands
- Somersaults over 6-inch object
- Walks line – heel toe
- Throws **9-inch ball** 12 to 13 feet
- Broad jumps 2 feet
- Jumps over **6-inch rope** with both feet
- Moves rhythmically to **music**
- Stands on tiptoes with hands on hips
- Touches toes with both hands
- Stands on one foot with arms folded across chest
- Stands on each foot alternately
- Swings each leg separately back and forth
- Walks up and kicks ball
- Hops forward on each foot separately
- Jumps backward
- Walks backward toe-to-heel
- Runs 35-yard dash
- Runs changing directions
- Jumps backward 6 times
- Bounces and catches large ball
- Draws simple recognizable pictures (house, man, tree)
- Cuts out and pastes simple shapes

PHYSICAL - FINE MOTOR

54 Months

- Copies simple word

60 Months

- Sharpens pencil
- Puts paperclip on paper
- Screws on one-inch lid
- Creases paper
- Cuts 6-inch square within one-fourth inch in 45 seconds

- Squeezes tube
- **Colors** within lines
- Crumples tissue paper into ball with one hand
- Makes recognizable objects out of **clay**

- Winds **thread** on **wooden spool**
- Inserts paper in ring binder
- Ties knot
- **Paints** recognizable picture
- Copies triangle
- Draws simple house
- Draws recognizable person with 6 to 7 body parts
- Cuts with scissors (under adult supervision) along a thick, straight or slightly curved line
- Copies first name

COGNITIVE

54 Months

- Repeats 4 digits
- Points to penny, nickel, dime
- Gives 3 objects
- Points to circle
- Points to triangle
- Counts by rote to 15

60 Months

- Picks longer line
- Points to elbows and ankles
- Copies a square
- Imitates 6-cube pyramid
- Completes **puzzles cut into several pieces**
- Sequentially orders 10 links of paper varying in size from large to small
- Remembers 2-step paper fold

- Reproduces simple sequential tapping patterns
- Repeats 4 digits
- Recites a poem from memory
- Identifies number concepts 2 and 3 (3 blocks from 10)
- Comprehends one-to-one correspondence with differing variables: (matching blocks to dots)
- Shifts categories when sorting shapes of different colors when cued (by shape first then by color)
- Matches domino patterns
- Matches simple **parquetry patterns**
- Tries to cut simple shapes
- Matches letter and number cards
- Imitates tapping pattern
- Points to sets that have 'more'
- Points to picture of first in line
- Names 3 coins
- Matches numerals 1 through 10
- Points to set with less
- Points to square
- Points to rectangle
- Points to 8 colors
- Names and tells use of clock
- Tells what's missing when 1 object is removed from group of 3
- Names first, middle and last positions

LANGUAGE

54 Months

- Tells use of senses
- Tells opposites
- Tells what common things are made of
- Uses compound sentences

60 Months

- Produces loud and soft sounds

- Locates "above," "below," "behind"
- Selects objects by comparative adjective (big, bigger, biggest)
- Reads numerals to 3
- Has increased vocabulary
- Uses 4- or 5-word sentences (usually correct grammar and subject)
- Uses compound and complex sentences
- Points to 8 body parts
- Tells definition of concrete nouns
- Names source of 15 actions
- Tells a story using pictures
- Rhymes words
- Follows 3-step directions in proper sequence
- Uses irregular plurals
- Gets person or item requested when asked
- Delivers 2-part verbal message

<u>SELF CARE</u>

54 Months (4 ½ years old)

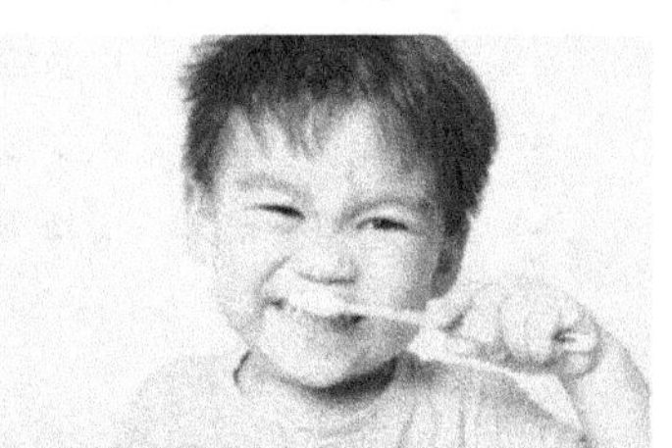

- Wash and dry face
- Inserts belt in loops
- Zips front zipper

60 Months (5 years old)

- Puts on pull-over garments
- Blows nose
- Prepares sandwich
- Undresses and dresses completely without assistance
- Cleans up spills getting own cloth
- Avoids poisons and all harmful substances
- Clears place at table
- Uses correct utensils for food
- Wakes from sleep during night to use toilet or stays dry all night

- Bathes self except for back, neck, and ears
- Serves self at table, parent holds serving dish
- Helps set table by correctly placing plates, napkins, and utensils with verbal cues
- Goes to bathroom in time, undresses, wipes self, flushes toilet, and dresses unaided
- Combs or brushes long hair
- Hangs up clothes on hanger
- Ties shoes

SOCIAL - EMOTIONAL

54 Months (4 ½ years old)

- Calls attention to own performance

60 Months (5 years old)

- Occupies self unattended
- Says "excuse me" appropriately
- Tells street and town in address
- Tells month of birth
- Chooses own friends
- Plays competitive exercise games
- Names and acts out three emotions
- Asks for assistance when having difficulty (with bathroom or getting a drink)
- Contributes to adult conversation
- Repeats rhymes, songs, or dances for others
- Works alone at chore for 10 to 15 minutes
- Apologizes without reminder 75% of the time
- Will take turns with 8 or 9 other children
- Plays with 2 or 3 children for 20 minutes in cooperative activity (project or game)
- Engages in socially acceptable behavior in public
- Asks permission to use objects belonging to others 75% of the time.

<u>**SPIRITUAL**</u>

Each Spiritual Section starts with several Scriptures to say aloud every night and memorize.

*"And whatever you ask in prayer (*according to God's will), believing, you will receive..."* Matthew 21:22 (NASB)

*Insert added for use as a teachable moment.

"And now faith, hope, and love remain, these three; but the greatest of these is love." 1 Corinthians 13:13 (NASB)

"Above all else, guard your heart, for everything you do flows from it." Proverbs 4:23 Use this scripture to teach that it is important not to see (on a screen, for example) or hear things that are scary or unwholesome. They may stay in your mind forever.

"What time I am afraid, I will trust in Thee." Psalm 56:3 (KJV)

"For we walk by faith, not by sight." 2 Corin 5: 7 (NASB)

At this age, children have a growing sense that God is very real and special. They sense that God loves and cares for them. They are developing attitudes of love and trust in Him.

- Puts hands together and says short prayer at dinner or bedtime (parent may now want to repeat the child's prayer phrase by phrase)
- Watches Listener Kids on YouTube with an adult and memorizes Scripture
- Listens to Bible story from Children's Bible Stories or other similar book
- Engages in dramatic play acting out Bible stories
- Repeats positive affirmations with parent
- Joins AWANA, American Heritage Girls, or Trail Life at 5 years of age
- Learns how to be sure if he will go to Heaven using **Five Fingers (below)**

Five Fingers*

1. **God loves me!** (Point to your thumb.) John 3:16 says "God so loved the world." This includes everyone, including you and me.

2. **I am a sinner.** (Point to your pointer finger.) Romans 3:23 says, "All have sinned." That means everyone sins except for Jesus. Romans 3:23 says that the penalty for sin is death, or eternal punishment in hell for sins. That is not good news, but there is good news!

3. **Jesus died for me.** (Point to your middle finger.) That is good news! 1 Corinthians 15:3-4 tells us that Jesus died on the cross and was raised on the third day to pay the penalty for our sins. Jesus loves us so-o-o much that He died on the cross for our sins.

4. **If I believe.** (Point to ring finger.) Ephesians 2:8-9 tells us that our path to everlasting life, living with God forever, is only through faith. It is a free gift, not something that we can earn. We are invited to believe in Jesus and repent of our sins.

5. **I can go to heaven.** (Point to pinky.) John 3:16 says that "whoever believes in Him should not perish but have everlasting life. That means when we die, we will live in heaven with God forever!"

When you are ready, you can pray a prayer asking God to forgive your sins and asking Jesus into your heart to save you from sin and to guide you each day!

Sings songs like "If You're Happy and You Know It" or "Peace Like a River" and "Rejoice in the LORD!" with your preschooler. Discuss a 'happy attitude' is a choice each day. We must take our thoughts captive and replace them with scripture as necessary. (For example: *"What time I am afraid, I will trust in Thee."* Psalm 56:3 (KJV)

With family around the table at mealtime, read Scripture aloud and discuss it with everyone saying something. In order to help children develop a biblical worldview and believe that every word of scripture is true, it is important to read every word of Scripture at some point. Even include Rahab the harlot (maybe not being too graphic about the discussion details until children are older) who is in the lineage of Jesus. Check out other colorful characters, as well.

Also, the Crucifixion of Jesus is rather graphic, but it is in the Bible, so it is appropriate to read and discuss that the purpose of the Crucifixion was the resurrection! **Jesus is Alive!**

We want our children prepared to face and stand up to the realities of our world. We must discuss these at home before children will face them in the world. Ask your children what they believe about controversial topics (like changing genders, evolution, climate change, etc.).

Let them practice answering and researching at home, before they confront these harsh realities in the world. We are to be **IN** the world, but not **OF** the world. We cannot expect our children to know how to handle such topics that are rampant everywhere if we shelter them. If we never expose them to what the world's point of view is versus our Christian biblical world view, they won't know how to respond.

Note to Parents:

It is time to set YOUR goals as parents and list on paper what you want to teach your children before they leave home and go to college, enlist in the military, or enter a career. See the book **"50 THINGS Every Child Should Know Before Leaving Home"** by Dr. Josh and Jen Mulvihill.

Other Suggested Activities: Children this age like to learn about and pretend they are different careers, like to dress up as a firefighter, a police officer, a doctor, or chef. Keep remnants of material or dress-up clothes in a bin or basket to aid the imagination for such creative play. For example, they can use one of Mom's old aprons with a homemade chef cap, a dish towel over his arm, and a spoon to be a chef. Watch a short, related YouTube video or Blippi about a career in action. Pick a career that starts with the letter of the alphabet that the child is learning that week.

Make a wall chart, or type one on the computer and print/post it on the wall, listing:

A for _______ B for _______ etc. Then fill in with a career (A is for Astronaut) or an object that starts with the letter that he is learning each week.

Use mealtime discussions so everyone can suggest careers. Stir up their thinking and creative juices!!

Parenting Tips:

The 4- to 5-year-old can clean up their toys or bedroom before bedtime or whatever time seems appropriate. If he is old enough to pick up something, he is old enough to help put away toys. Stand firm on these rules. Tell him with firmness. Expect results.

Provide a labeled cubby or bin for each type of toy. Label each bin, drawer, and cubby with a picture (by laying out a few of the toys that go in that drawer and taking a picture to print out) and 1 to 2 words to label each cubby.

For example, a plastic drawer might have pictures of the child's toy cars and trucks with the words *Cars* taped to the front of the drawer. The parent would say, "Let's put the cars and trucks in the Cars drawer."

Sometimes a child may need help or reminding to straighten up, but generally, he can put things up without assistance by this age. Be aware of the stall tactics or excuses like having to go to the restroom, asking for food, or suddenly being too tired.

As a reward, he can receive words of praise and thank you. Occasionally, offer a healthy treat like raisins, but don't let children plot to put away ONLY if they get a prize or treat. Living in a safe, happy home means EVERYONE chips in on the work!! **It's the beginning of teaching/learning a work ethic.**

GIFT IDEAS:

NOTE the <u>underlined</u> and <u>boldfaced</u> items in developmental lists.
More gift ideas in the **GIFT IDEAS** section at the end of the chapter.

- Children's poem book
- Dominoes
- Paint with brushes and paper
- Dress-up clothes for different careers
- Simple board games like Chutes and Ladders
- Kitchen Science book (My Heavenly Father curriculum)
- Pegs and peg board for counting and simple addition or subtraction (from My Heavenly Father curriculum)

NOTE: It is more important to create memories together than give gifts.

Books as Gifts:

Boyack, Connor & Stanfield, Elijah, The Tuttle Toddlers <u>The 1 2 3s of the Bill of Rights</u>, (5-11 years) <u>https://tuttletwins.com/products</u>.

Boyack, Connor & Stanfield, Elijah, The Tuttle Toddlers <u>The A B Cs of the American Revolution</u>, (5–11 years) <u>https://tuttletwins.com/products</u>.

Cameron, Kirk, <u>As You Grow</u>, Brave Books, Dec. 1, 2022. (#1 in Children's Christian Values Fiction)

<u>Otto's Tales: The National Anthem and the Pledge of Allegiance,</u> by Prager U, April11, 2022.

St. Clair, Ashley, <u>Elephants Are Not Birds</u>, Brave Books, January 1, 2021. (for 4-12 years)

If you need help for yourself and your children to be able to take a stand for your family's Christian values in education and in the world, contact us for a free 1-on-1 Strategy Session: <u>*edempower777@gmail.com*</u>

Education Empowerment Coach
Susan Perez

BIBLIOGRAPHY

Bleck, Eugene E. and Donald A. Nagel. "Functional Development Assessment." <u>Physically Handicapped Children: A Medical Atlas for Teachers.</u> New York: Grune & Stratton.

Bluma, S., and others. "Portage Guide to Early Education," Portage Project, CESA12. Portage, Wisconsin: Cooperative Education Service Agency 12.

Children's Bureau Blog "Why the First 5 Years of Child Development Are So Important," 09/25/2018. <u>https://www.all4kids.org/news</u>.

"Doctor Visits – Take Care of Your Child's Teeth," <u>www.health.gov/MyHealthFinder/doctor-visits/regular-checkups/take-care-your-childs-teeth</u>. Updated Nov. 4, 2022.

Furuno, Setsu, and others. <u>Hawaii Early Learning Profile (HELP) Activity Guide.</u> Palo Alto, California: VORT Corporation.

Gesell, Arnold, M.D. <u>The First Five Years of Life.</u> New York: Harper & Brothers Publishers.

House, Polly, "Want Your Church to Grow?" Baptist Press, April 3, 2003. <u>https://www.baptistpress.com/resources-library/news</u>

La Leche League <u>https://llli.org/breastfeeding-info/back-to-breast/</u>

Langley, Beth. "Developmental Guidelines for Teachers and Evaluators of Multi-handicapped Children," George Peabody College for Teachers.

*Mulvihill, Dr. Josh. "Discipling Your Grandchildren, Great Ideas to Help Them Know, Love, and Serve God," Bethany House Publishers, 2020.

Phipps, Abbey, "Raising Jesus Kids,"
https://raisingjesuskids.com/raising-jesus-kids/ March 3, 2021.

Sanford, Anne R. and Janet G. Zelman. "LAP – The Learning
Accomplishment Profile (Revised Edition)," Winston-Salem, North
Carolina: Kaplan Press.

Special Education Department, Dallas I.S.D. "Kids Inventory of
Developmental Scale," Dallas, Texas.

Smith, Robert M. and John T. Neisworth. The Exceptional Child.
New York: McGraw-Hill Book Co.

"What are the Milestones for the 4- 5-Year-Old Child?" , by Medical
Author: Karthik Kumar, MBBS, Medicine Net, 06/25/2021,
https://www.medicinenet.com/milestones_for_a_4-_to_5-year-
old_child/article.htm.

Why the First 5 Years of Child Development Are So Important, Blog,
09/25/2018, www.all4kids.org

ACKNOWLEDGEMENTS

First, I give all glory to God for creating and developing this book.

Then, I gratefully acknowledge that I learned how to write a book through the excellent instruction, guidance, and prayers at Kingdom Builders Academy – specifically Coaches Rae Lynn Johnson, David Baker, Sioux Smith, Andy DeWitt, Chonta Hayes, and Carol Fairman along with my Wednesday morning team.

Also, a big thank you to Marilyn Murfee for tirelessly reading and making corrections as my editor.

Thank you, my friend and spiritual contributor Lana Burson.

Great appreciation for my sister, Jackie, who has been excited and supportive and given me confidence from the beginning.

Last and most (not least), thank you to my family, especially my children and grandchildren, and friends, each of whom provided support, encouragement, and the "real-life" stories, wisdom, and love that are incorporated into this book.

THANKS and GRACE to each person who read this book in advance and helped make corrections and wrote reviews!

PRAISE GOD for Christian parents and grandparents and for my dad's Bible on the front cover of this book opened to Psalm 56:3, a Scripture we shared when I was young.

ABOUT THE AUTHOR

Christian. Caring. Dedicated. Determined. Experienced.

Susan Elaine Perez, an ***Education Empowerment Coach,*** teaches parents and students to stand firm for their family's Christian values in education and the world.

She **raised 3 children, helped raise 3 grandchildren**, and thousands of students over the years, along with lots of training, and research on best practices that work with children. She has **over 40 years of experience in education** as a **teacher, administrator, consultant**, and **superintendent.**

As school superintendent Perez:

- Focused on mastery of basic skills.

- Secured grant funding for 4 fine-arts teachers, that collaborated with elementary teachers weekly to plan and reinforce academic objectives.

- Increased parent involvement and individualized tutoring for struggling students.

- Implemented the ***Coca-Cola Valued Youth Program,*** where at-risk high school students were paid to each tutor three at-risk elementary students. This gave the high school students a review of skills and a modest income. The elementary students received weekly tutoring by a caring mentor.

As a result, **achievement test scores soared** from one-year-below grade level to one-year-above grade level in just 3 years!

Perez served as a State of Texas Higher Education Board Member for Health Sciences. With experience adopting textbooks, she investigates why many schools are no longer requiring textbooks, since the lack of hard-copy books greatly increases the possibility of indoctrination.

She was selected as **one of two Texas teachers** to attend the Health Science National Consortium and went on the following year to **present** at the **Health Science National Consortium**, where she shared an innovative unit called "Know Your Heart."

Perez believes the most critical needs in education right now are *parents' involvement* and *voicing their Christian values*.

Through **TAKE YOUR STAND Coaching**, Perez teaches 4 simple steps to empowerment:

- ***Ten Things to Know*** - provides excellent resources on Critical Race Theory, Social-Emotional Learning, Comprehensive Sex Education, Gender Confusion, and the truth about Separation of Church and State, etc.

- ***Ten Things to Say*** - empowers client's ability to stand up to intimidation and deception of our children, like David stood up to Goliath or Jesus' response to the money changers in the Temple.

- ***Ten Things to Do*** - each client picks his own project to take a stand for his Christian values in education, and with Susan's help, begins to make a difference.

- ***Ten Ways to Insulate their (Grand)children*** - from the indoctrination so prevalent in society today.

Perez's ability to give parents their voice in education creates life-altering outcomes, for her clients and their families, but also for those affected by these positive changes.

Call to Action: Contact *edempower777@gmail.com* *for help learning to take a* **stand for your family's Christian values** *and teaching your children and grandchildren to Stand for Truth.*